God, Action, and Embodiment

by

THOMAS F. TRACY

GRAND RAPIDS, MICHIGAN
WILLIAM B. EERDMANS PUBLISHING COMPANY

For Kathryn

255 Jefferson Ave. S.E., Grand Rapids, Mich. 49503

Printed in the United States of America

Library of Congress Cataloging in Publication Data

Tracy, Thomas F., 1948 -
God, action, and embodiment.

Revision of thesis (Ph. D.) — Yale University, 1980.
Includes index.
1. God. 2. Psychology, Religious. 3. Philosophical theology. 4. Mind and body. 5. Analogy (Religion)
I. Title.
BT102.T69 1983 231'.044 83-25498
ISBN 0-8028-1999-0

Contents

PART THREE **PERSONS AND THE DIVINE AGENT**

Introduction

Generation by generation, theologians have puzzled over the ways in which language must be hammered into a new shape when used in talk of God. As soon as we say, for example, that God bears a creative relation to our world, we must introduce some extraordinary qualifications. For God's creative activity, unlike our own, is not limited to reshaping a world that exists quite apart from his intentions for it. Rather God creates *ex nihilo;* his creative act accounts for the very existence of the creature. Or again, God is addressed as a personal being, yet theologians have been careful to add that God is not a person: God is not bodily in any familiar sense, not located in space and time, not composed of parts, not subject to change.

These peculiar combinations of affirmation and negation in theology can be quite perplexing. With characteristic vividness, Augustine gives us an account in his *Confessions* of his early struggles to conceive of a God who is both a personal will addressed in prayer and an unembodied spirit who transcends the spatiality of our world. The denial that God occupies *a* space (i.e., a body), coupled with the assertion that God is always present, suggested to Augustine the idea of a being uniformly distributed throughout the universe.

> Though I did not think of you in the shape of a human body, I was still forced to think of you as a corporeal substance occupying space. . . . I thought of you as an immensity through infinite space, interfused everywhere throughout the whole mass of the universe and extending beyond it in every direction for distances without end.[1]

But this conception would not do, for it entails that "the body of an elephant would contain more of [God] than the body of a sparrow to the extent that it is larger and occupies more space."[2] Augustine recognized that in his effort to envision omnipresence he had not overcome spatial thinking, but had simply spread God around more evenly. Yet even once he acknowledged this, he could think of God only by using spatial metaphors which he then carefully qualified.

> You fill heaven and the earth. Do they therefore contain you? Or after you have filled them, is there still something of you left over, since they are unable to contain you? . . . Or is it not rather the case that you have no need to be contained by anything? . . . You who fill everything are wholly present in everything which you fill. . . . Everywhere you are present in your entirety, and no single thing can contain you in your entirety.[3]

Augustine artfully "breaks" his spatial metaphor in just the way necessary to help us toward the idea of a being who is fully present in every place yet located in none.

In religious discourse the reflective imagination approaches its own limits. Theology is committed to speaking in an intelligible and responsible way of a reality it cannot fully grasp. If theologians are to speak of God at all, they must draw upon materials close at hand, modifying familiar concepts so as to propel thought in the direction they intend. Theological reflection, of course, is not the only domain of inquiry that is deeply indebted to a qualified transfer of patterns of thought from one context to another. The imagery of a poem and the explanatory model developed by a natural scientist both draw their penetrative power from a skillful recognition of likenesses. Thought about God, however, is both particularly dependent upon such techniques and particularly radical in the qualifications it places upon customary patterns of speech. Philosophers with a special interest in language have given a great deal of attention to these features of theological self-expression. But the suggestion that language is subject to special stresses when used in theology is not a modern insight. At least since the recovery of Aristotle in the twelfth century there has been a vigorous theological tradition of reflection upon the analogical capacities of language.

My project in this essay is to examine some of the key conceptual structures at work both in our familiar references to one another as persons and in our talk of God as a personal being. This way of putting things points to the dual focus of my study. My overarching interest is in the possibilities and problems inherent in efforts to conceive of God as One Who Acts (i.e., as an agent), the bearer of a personal identity made manifest in action. In order to address these issues in theology, I will take a careful look at the concepts of *character, action,* and *agency* at work in our references to persons. Our concepts of what it is to be a person are modified and put to work in a special way when we speak of God as a personal and purposive being. By attending to these familiar (though complex) concepts we can better understand the distinctive development they receive in theistic discourse. There are two interconnected advantages to be gained by such considerations. Critically, we can shed light on the special modifications that are made in these conceptual structures when they are put to work in theology. Constructively, we can explore the resources these concepts provide for aiding theological imagination in its task of speaking intelligibly about God.

Why single out concepts of character, action, and agency for special attention in theology? The simplest answer is that these concepts figure prominently in the religious traditions that have given rise to theological reflection. Reference to what God has done, is doing, and will do is obviously prominent in the biblical literature that nourishes Jewish and Christian theism. And within the primary language of religious life—the language of prayer and praise, exhortation and encouragement—images of God as a personal will have characteristically played an important role. God is addressed, for example, as the creator of all things, who brings human life into being and intends that it be fulfilled in relation to himself. God is said to shape the course of human affairs, both great and small, so that this intention for his creature's well-being can be realized. This is a drama worked out both in individual lives and in the histories of communities. God acts in the history of Israel, establishing his covenant with Abraham, empowering Moses to liberate his people, raising up priests and prophets, and struggling with human faithlessness. In the fullness of time God joins us in fellow-humanity in Jesus Christ and overcomes the terror of human estrangement from God. The recital of these events calls attention to God's continuing activity shaping lives in accordance with his creative purposes.

Not all Christians speak in just these ways. This pattern of religious affirmation is hardly a normative summary of Christian doctrine. But these forms of expression (or others very like them) appear again and again throughout the history of Christianity. They are typical enough that theologians seeking to understand the persistent themes that shape religious life must come to terms with them in one way or another. In doing so, they must deal with the contention that God is a personal being who acts purposefully in relation to humankind. The God referred to in these ways is not primarily a component part of a grand metaphysical scheme, an abstraction belonging to an inclusive theoretical picture of reality; rather, he is a decisively important actor within a drama that embraces the whole of our world and each of us in particular. Who this agent is becomes apparent in what he has done, in those deeds in which he has displayed his intention toward the predicament and destiny of humankind. And on the basis of these actions he is characterized as just, loving, and wise, and perhaps also as wrathful and jealous.

The prominence of these patterns of religious expression makes clear the theological relevance of my focus upon character, action, and agency. The concept of God as an agent whose actions engage humankind in a decisively important way is unquestionably a fundamental strand in Western theistic traditions. But it is important to note that I am not claiming that this is the only pattern of reference to God at work in the primary language of religious faith. Nor am I claiming that a Christian theologian must unavoidably give concepts of action and agency a central role in his reflection upon God, though that is what I propose to do here. The imagery of divine action and purpose is deeply rooted in the language by which the Christian communities have lived, but there are other tendencies at work in theistic discourse as well. Particularly if considered over any stretch of its history, the language of religious life is dynamic, diverse, and occasionally inconsistent. A broad array of expressive patterns, rooted in the authoritative sources of communal identity (e.g., Scriptures, creeds, honored theological documents), provide the context for theological reflection and the content that such reflection seeks to understand.

Theology is inevitably selective, developing some of the tendencies at work in the primary discourse of religious life and passing others by. As a result, claims to have captured *the* Christian understanding of God must be greeted with a degree of skepticism. Theologians attempt to identify (and/or introduce) an intelligible order in the great body of stories, images, doctrines, stock expressions, and so on that appear in a religious tradition. Their task is to generate a structure of thought that draws out and elaborates the interconnected meanings present in a vast network of expressive practices. Given the diversity within their sources, they may sacrifice richness for the sake of unified intelligibility. For this reason, an important part of evaluating a theological proposal is the assessment of its adequacy in measuring up to the complexity of the materials available in the religious tradition. Systematic consistency may sometimes be less highly prized in theology than the ability to provide a place for enduring (even if conflicting) tendencies in religious self-expression.

It is important, then, to acknowledge the limits of this project. I want to explore the conceptual underpinnings of a particular (and, I believe, particularly important) set of themes in theistic discourse. It may be that concentration upon the language of divine action, will, and purpose needs to be weighed in the balance against certain other emphases in any thematically adequate doctrine of God. But my project here is limited to exploring the possibilities for organizing our thought about God relative to the affirmation that he is one who acts. I want to pursue this possibility as far as I can, laying bare the conceptual structures upon which it depends and following out the logic of these structures as consistently as possible. I will not try to prove that God is an agent or argue that this is *the* correct way to conceive of God. I am not setting out to show, for example, that this systematic emphasis most faithfully interprets biblical materials, most completely appropriates theological tradition, or most adequately articulates the themes of religious experience. Broader questions about the theological usefulness of this approach must in any case wait until we see where it leads us. I do want to show, however, that a way of conceiving of God as an agent is available for theological use; we can, I will argue, formulate such a proposal coherently and develop it with a significant degree of clarity and detail. In the process, I hope to illustrate the fruitfulness of giving concepts of agency and action a fundamental role in structuring theological reflection.[4] My project can be expressed as a thought experiment. If we fix our attention upon the volitional themes in theistic discourse and give them a central place in theological construction, what shape will this give our concept of God?

Among twentieth-century theologians there has been persistent interest in the personalistic and volitional themes in Christian self-expression. Theologians as varied as Karl Barth, Charles Hartshorne, and Austin Farrer have, in their different ways, stressed the primacy of love and the centrality of will in understanding the nature of God.[5] The concern to give these concepts an important place in theological reflection has complex roots. In some instances it has been tied to a broad-based modern reaction against the frozen elegance of medieval metaphysics. Hartshorne has articulately called attention to what he perceives to be the isolated perfection and religious inaccessibility of the God of classical theism. In other circles, this shift in theological categories has been linked to a reassessment of scriptural narrative. In this regard one thinks particularly of the "biblical theologians."[6] In conscious contrast to the pattern of liberal theology since Schleiermacher, these theologians have held to a doctrine of unique historical revelation through God's self-declaring actions. Knowledge of God, they have argued, is not grounded in any universal human capacity, whether rational or affective; rather, God is known through the particular acts in which he shapes the history of Israel and redeems all of humankind. Divine action in human history becomes the medium of revelation, and the content of revelation is the personal disclosure that takes place through these actions. God's mighty acts in history constitute a *Heilsgeschichte* in which his nature and intentions are made known to us.

Views of this sort have been profoundly influential in twentieth-century Protestant theology. It was widely felt in the biblical theology movement that they had recovered the authentic scriptural message and that it could henceforth be used as the source and norm for contemporary theological work. They were far too sanguine in this supposition. The factors involved in evaluating the adequacy of a theological proposal to Scripture and tradition are considerably more complex than is acknowledged by an appeal simply to "the biblical view."[7] There can be little question, however, that biblical theologians who have emphasized the revelation of God's purposes in action have expressed *a* biblically well-grounded and important view.

Biblical theology has crumbled under a number of pressures. Not the least of these was the inability of biblical theologians to explain some of their own basic concepts adequately, as Langdon Gilkey has pointed out in a particularly telling article.[8] The biblical theologians depended heavily on scriptural language about God's actions in human history, and yet they were unwilling to take the biblical stories at face value. A Christian knows God as he who freed the Hebrew people from slavery in Egypt. But many modern Christians doubt that there were miraculous plagues, parted waters, and pillars of fire. What then are they celebrating when they proclaim God's mighty acts in history? We can hardly announce triumphantly that God has made himself known through his actions in history if we find ourselves unable to say what the divine agent has done. Clearly a more detailed account is needed of what it means to say that God is an agent who acts in relation to man and nature. But this is a task for which the biblical theologian, by virtue of his own conception of theological method, was ill-equipped. In the *locus classicus* of biblical theology, G. E. Wright argues that the theological enterprise in any generation consists of reexpressing the biblical message in contemporary language.[9] His supposition is that "the biblical message" has a readily identified content that is independent of any particular expressive strategy in theology. But this supposition collapses if it turns out that the biblical message takes on a definite shape only within the interpretive and expressive categories of particular theological proposals (e.g., about God's relation as an agent to the events of human history).

Since the waning of biblical theology, there have been a number of efforts to deal with the problems it brought into focus. I will not try to review this literature here except to note an underlying pattern that appears in two of the best known of these discussions. Both Schubert Ogden and Gordon Kaufman have offered a response to the question that Gilkey pressed so effectively against bibilical theology, namely, "What does it mean to speak of an act of God in history?"[10] There are three points I want to make about their proposals.

First, their fundamental strategies in responding to Gilkey are parallel. Both draw back from saying that God does in fact act *in* history (i.e., that God seeks specific ends in particular historical events) and emphasize instead God's enactment *of* history (as a whole). That is, both theologians answer the question about God's action in history by offering an account of God's general activity in relation to natural and historical processes. Given such an account, they can then ask what it might mean to say that certain events embody or reveal God's wider purposes in a special way.

Second, in constructing an account of God's general activity, each theologian employs certain key analogies drawn from his understanding of the human agent. Ogden suggests that we think of God's relation to the world as analogous to the relation of mind, or self, to the body. The self, Ogden tells us, is constituted fundamentally by inner acts of decision in which it determines the particular character of its relation to its world. "It is only because the self first acts to constitute itself, to respond to its world, and to decide its own inner being that it 'acts' at all in the more ordinary meaning of the word."[11] These inner decisions are the primary sense in which the self acts: "outer acts of word and deed are but ways of expressing and implementing the inner decisions whereby it constitutes itself as the self."[12] Bodily actions "re-present" in a public way the private resolves of the self. Drawing upon this understanding of the embodied self, Ogden contends that God's action "is not an action in history but an action which transcends it."[13] For God's act, in the primary sense, is the ever-renewed determination of the content of his own life as a harmony of loving relationships to creatures. At every moment God "constitutes himself as God by participating fully and completely in the world of his creatures, thereby laying the ground for the next stage of the creative process."[14] History, in the widest possible sense (i.e., the world process), expresses God's own continuous self-enactment.

Kaufman rejects the analogy of divine embodiment in the world. But Kaufman's proposal, like Ogden's, trades upon a distinction between the self as we have access to it in bodily action and the self as the deciding center of personal life. "What one directly experiences of the other are, strictly speaking, the external physical sights and sounds he makes, not the deciding, acting, purposing center of the self."[15] Though we do not have direct access to the agent-self, we do take these physical sights and sounds to be deeds and words that disclose a personal reality lying beyond the limits of perceptual experience. Here, Kaufman claims, we have a familiar instance of a personal reality that transcends that which is given in sense experience. This provides a model for God's relation to history: God is an agent whose purposes lie behind and are revealed within the outer "sights and sounds" of human history. We cannot say that God acts for particular ends within our world since that, Kaufman argues, would violate the modern understanding of our world as an autonomous and self-contained whole.[16] But we can say that history as a whole is God's "master act." To say that God acts is to say that the "whole complicated and intricate teleological movement of all nature and history should be regarded as a single all-encompassing act of God."[17]

The third point I would like to make regarding the positions of Ogden and Kaufman is that the most powerful criticisms that have been offered of their proposals have been aimed at their anthropological foundations. The analogies that organize these schemes clearly presuppose a number of important claims about the human agent, and it is these presuppositions that have been challenged. The disconcerting thrust of such criticism is that the person concepts at work in these proposals are philosophically problematic at just those points where they appear to be most useful theologically.

Ogden's proposal, for example, depends upon an understanding of the self as (a) separate from and interacting with the body, and (b) a hidden reality whose overt actions are merely the secondary expression of its inner self-determination. It is precisely claims of this sort that have come in for sustained criticism in contemporary philosophy of mind. Without further explanation (which Ogden indicates is necessary but which he does not supply), these claims appear to trade upon a flat-footed mind-body dualism.[18] Ogden's views, however, should not be labeled crypto-Cartesian too quickly; rather, they should be read against the background of Whitehead's metaphysical categories and evaluated in light of the special appeal and puzzlement that attaches to that scheme.[19] But in any case, the anthropological underpinnings of Ogden's analogies must be worked out more fully before his theological proposal will come into focus clearly.

Similar criticisms have been made of Kaufman's efforts. His claim that persons elude one another's cognitive grasp and can be known only as they freely disclose themselves has provoked the charge of "residual Cartesianism."[20] That is, Kaufman's proposal seems to trade upon claims about the privacy and inaccessibility of selves that presuppose a discredited Cartesian understanding of persons—and indeed it is hard to see how his proposal can be made to work without this problematic privacy of the self.

A great deal more might be said about these two schemes, both in criticism and defense. We might argue at length, for example, about whether the criticisms that I have mentioned are justified, whether these proposals can be adjusted to accommodate them, and so on. But the point I wish to underscore here is that this ongoing debate will turn at least in part upon certain general claims about the concept of a person. Insofar as theologians make such claims, disputes about theological proposals will intersect with contemporary discussion in philosophy of mind and theory of action. In particular, the very powerful critique that contemporary Anglo-American philosophy has directed at mind-body dualism will have a significant impact on the way in which such theological discussions will unfold, for if we are persuaded to abandon views that divide persons into inaccessible minds and publicly observable bodies, then the fund of analogical material available to the theologian will change in an important way. Both Ogden and Kaufman seem to trade on a strong distinction (though not necessarily the same distinction) between the agent and his body as the basis for talk of a God who can be distinguished from the world but who acts upon or through it. But if this picture of the agent as an entity distinct from the body is given up, can we any longer extract theologically useful analogies from our person concepts? Indeed, we may wonder whether embodiment plays so crucial a role in the concept of an agent that being a body (as opposed to being merely contingently associated with a body) is a necessary condition for being an agent. Precisely this has been confidently claimed by some of the philosophical critics of theism. Paul Edwards states this point nicely:

> What does it mean to speak of a pure spirit, a disembodied mind, as infinitely (or finitely) powerful, wise, good, just, and all the rest? . . . What would it be like to be, for example, just, without a body? To be just, a person has to behave in certain ways. But how is it possible to perform these acts, to behave in the required ways, without a body? . . . These questions are of course inspired by the conviction . . . that it does not make sense to talk about a disembodied consciousness, that psychological predicates are logically tied to the behavior of organisms. . . . However much more than a body a human being may be, one cannot sensibly talk about this "more" without presupposing (as part of what one means, and not as a mere contingent fact) that he is a living organism.[21]

Commenting on these questions about agency and embodiment,

W. D. Hudson remarks that "this is the point at which the shoe pinches hardest for anyone who wishes to offer a philosophical defence of religious belief in general and theism in particular."[22]

All of this suggests that particular interpretive proposals about God's actions in history must wait upon a clarification of fundamental issues surrounding both the concept of an agent and the use of this concept to structure our understanding of God. Our answer to questions about God's active relation to the world will be tied to our way of conceiving of agents generally and to the possibilities this opens up for conceiving of the divine agent in particular. Once these issues have been clarified, the answer to Gilkey's question will appear within the detail of a fully developed doctrine of God.

My efforts here will not in fact be directed to working out a detailed response to Gilkey's question. There are any number of different ways of developing an account of God's activity in relation to our world, and these are typically tied to other features of one's theological position. For example, what a theologian says about whether and how God acts within human history will be quite closely connected to his Christology. For the purposes of this discussion, I want to leave open as many particular doctrinal options as possible. My aim is to clarify underlying structures of thought, to make conceptual resources available for theological construction, and to sketch the central structures of one or more ways of putting these resources to work in conceiving of a God who acts. A fully developed doctrine of God—one that has been carefully set in relation to other doctrinal issues—must make a great many choices that are not and should not be made on the basis of a study of this kind. But unless we are clear and self-conscious about the structures of thought we employ in theology, there is little prospect of producing a doctrine of God that is either conceptually sound or theologically satisfying.

It will be useful to have before us a brief account of the skeletal structure of the discussion that follows. My study is divided into three parts. Part One (Chaps. 1-2) explores fundamental conceptual structures at work in our familiar references to persons. The argument in these chapters has a deductive organization. Chapter 1 opens with an examination of the language we use in telling *who* a person is—that is, in characterizing him or her as the bearer of a unique personal identity. This vocabulary of "character traits" lies at the heart of the rest of my study, for it is this vocabulary that gives content to the concept of a personal being, whether human or divine. The central claim of Chapter 1 is that in ascribing traits of character we identify enduring patterns in the intentional action of an agent. If we are to say that God is loving or just, we must be prepared to say that God is an agent whose actions can be characterized in these ways.

Chapter 2 turns to the concept of intentional action in greater detail. What do we mean when we say that a person acts on purpose, or intentionally? In the process of answering this question and sifting through the philosophical issues that surround it, the central structures of the concept of an agent come into focus.

Part Two (Chaps. 3-4) and Part Three (Chaps. 5-7) examine two different ways of developing the concept of an agent and explore the implications of these views for constructive theological reflection.

The two chapters in Part Two focus on mind-body dualism and its theological correlates. Chapter 3 briefly introduces Descartes's proposals and key distinctions, considers the principal points at which this view has been attacked, and explores the consequences for theology of giving up the central categories of Cartesian dualism. Mind-body dualism holds out some promising possibilities for use in theology. If we reject this analysis of the human agent, how serious a blow is dealt to the project of conceiving of God as an agent? The most obvious problem concerns embodiment: do our arguments against dualism lead to the conclusion that a necessary condition for being an agent is being a body (i.e., a psychophysical unit)?

Chapter 4 takes up a powerful argument against mind-body dualism that appears to warrant this broader conclusion. The argument, authored by Peter Strawson, hinges on the claim that a noncorporeal personal being cannot be picked out uniquely as an item of unambiguous reference. I argue that there are a number of ways in which God can be identified, even within the terms of Strawson's discussion. Among these is a mode of identification that relies upon God's unique relation to those events that we take to be his actions. Identifying reference to God, however, depends upon a supporting context provided by a network of auxiliary claims about our world (a "theistic story").

Part Three develops a non-Cartesian understanding of the human agent and explores the ways in which this conception of persons might be used in theology. Chapter 5 works out an account of the human agent as a complex psychophysical unit, giving special attention to the role of the body as the basis and medium of our activity as agents.

Chapter 6 puts this concept of the person to work in theology, experimenting with nondualistic forms of the suggestion (from Hartshorne, Ogden, and others) that God be thought of as embodied in the world. I consider some of the liabilities of such proposals and conclude that there is no compelling reason to say that God is a bodily agent.

Chapter 7 then develops the fundamental structures of a constructive proposal in which embodiment is denied of God precisely in order to affirm the perfection of his agency. A human agent can prescribe the pattern of his own activity only within limits established by a structure of bodily life that he does not choose or intentionally enact. If we affirm the completeness of God's self-determination, then we must deny that God is embodied in this sense. The capacity for intentional self-regulation, which is necessarily a property of any agent, is radicalized and completed in the divine agent. A similar point can be made about the completeness of God's unity and power. In God's life, then, the capacities that define agency find their perfect expression. This proposal maps out a path between two of the most sharply opposed options in contemporary discussion of the doctrine of God. On the one hand, it stands with the tradition of classical theism (as expressed by Thomas Aquinas and his interpreters) in maintaining that God exists from himself (*a se*) in sovereign independence from the world. On the other hand, it joins process theology (as expressed by various theological interpreters of Alfred North Whitehead) in affirming that God enters into mutually affecting relations of profound love and shared destiny with his creatures.

Acknowledgments

A thought project of this kind takes shape in a context of reflection and conversation to which many people contribute. The richness of that conversation is a gift one receives from the intellectual efforts of others. I want especially to thank David Kelsey, who advised this project when it was a doctoral dissertation at Yale University and who read multiple versions of these ideas with unfailing perceptiveness and critical clarity. In addition, William Christian, Hans Frei, and Gene Outka provided valuable comment and counsel as the text developed. Nancy Gerth took the time to give the text a careful reading at an important stage. I also want to thank the members of the Theology Group for their attention to these ideas and their vigorous work on related themes.

PART ONE

Character and Action

CHAPTER 1

Traits of Character

1. CHARACTER TRAIT PREDICATES

If theologians are to speak of God as a personal being, then they must draw upon the descriptive vocabulary we use in characterizing each other as persons. In this chapter we will consider some of the conceptual structures at work in the language we use in speaking of that which is distinctively personal about persons.

We often want to know who a person is beyond simply knowing his or her name. This usually amounts to asking, "Can you 'place' this person for me?"—that is, can you place this person in a sphere of activity and influence that I can recognize (e.g., as mayoral candidate, owner of the local hardware store, etc.)? But frequently this is not enough. We want to know who the person is in a richer sense, and so might go on to ask, "What is he like?" In this case we are seeking information that will give us some sense of his characteristic patterns of action and emotion. We are hoping for some insight into this person as a distinctive individual.

In order to satisfy such a request, we often say something about what that person has done. We tell a story the point of which can be expressed by saying that the actions narrated in the story display the person's characteristic energy or ambition or wisdom or avarice or the like. The characterizing term directs attention to particular features of the story, suggesting that it be viewed in a certain light. The story, in turn, fills out the detail of the characterization, giving it concreteness. In making the general statement that a particular person is "clever but not wise," for example, we establish only certain rough expectations for that person's behavior. But if this description is accompanied by a story of a typical situation and behavior in which this characteristic is displayed, then we learn something about the distinctive way this person fails to be wise in his cleverness.

In the discussion that follows I will argue for a necessary logical relation between a crucial set of predicates used in characterizing persons and "stories" that treat human behavior as *intentional* action. That is, I will argue that certain distinctively person-characterizing predicates can only be ascribed on the basis of the intentional actions of an agent.

The class of predicates I will consider could be given any number of labels, each misleading in its own way. Let us designate them as "character traits." This class of character traits will be quite diverse. First, it will include traits of moral character (e.g., courage, love, wisdom, generosity, vanity, greed, etc.); second, it will include a wide range of general personality traits that do not carry explicitly moral connotations (e.g., pleasantness, good humor, hostility, practicality, aggressiveness, etc.); and third, it will include a range of predicates that might be called qualities of intellect—predicates that constitute the vocabulary through which the concept of intelligence is exercised in particular assessments of behavior (e.g., cleverness, acuity, dullness, orderliness, etc.).

These rough groupings are not intended to identify hard-and-fast distinctions between sub-sets of character traits. Any number of different groupings might be made. Their purpose is rather to identify some representative traits of character and suggest a strategy for identifying others. I will not try to fix exact boundaries for this class of predicates; that would require a precise specification of the sufficient conditions for membership in the class. But I do want to articulate one of the necessary conditions for counting a predicate as a trait of character: I will argue that character trait predicates require that any behavior they are used to appraise be *intentional* action and any individual they are used to characterize be an *agent*.[1] There are, of course, a large number of predicates used in describing persons that do not satisfy this condition—"has blue eyes," "is twenty pounds overweight," and so on. And there are even a number of predicates used in answering questions about what persons "are like" that do not satisfy this condition: predicates like "fidgety," "sickly," "breaks out in a rash when nervous," and so on describe a person in terms of what he is liable to undergo rather than in terms of what he characteristically undertakes.

My argument in this chapter will turn upon three points about the logic of character trait predicates. First, these predicates can be used both to appraise particular behaviors and to characterize the individual who displays those behaviors. Second, a statement ascribing a character trait to an individual entails that it has been appropriate in the past and/or will be appropriate in the future to appraise some of that individual's behavior in this way; the use of these predicates to appraise particular behaviors is in this sense "logically basic." And third, these predicates are used to appraise behavior described as the intentional action of an agent.

2. APPRAISALS OF BEHAVIOR AND OF CHARACTER

The first of these points distinguishes two related uses of character trait predicates. We often evaluate particular things that persons do as wise or kind or generous, and so on. Sometimes we go on to say that the person whose behavior we have appraised this way can himself be characterized as wise or kind or generous. One may appraise as generous John's offer of help to a distressed friend. And one might be led by this to say that John is a generous person. In appraising John's offer as generous we evaluate a particular episode; in characterizing John as a generous person we pick out an enduring trait of character.

A word is in order here about the use of character trait predicates to appraise, or evaluate, particular actions.[2] It is important to note that these terms tell us relatively little about any particular action unless they are supported by a materially more detailed description. If we are told that John's action was generous we still have a lot to find out about it. From this laudatory remark we do not even learn what in fact he did, and this we need to know both in order to appreciate the force of "generous" in this instance and in order to make our own judgment about whether his action really was generous. While it is notoriously difficult to draw any neat distinction between description and evaluation, some form of that distinction seems to be called for here. Character trait predicates appraise behavior taken under a description in which the evaluative predicate does not appear (for that would beg the question) but on which our evaluation is a commentary (about which we might disagree). We appraise John's action taken under a description of its relevant content and context. Our evaluation does not add a further detail to this description. In assessing John's behavior as generous we do not note an additional activity beyond that which we have described as his offer of help. Rather, on the basis of the description of John's behavior that we have before us, we make a judgment that bears with varying emphasis on the motives displayed in it, on the style of its performance, on the quality of its achievement.

One of the consequences of this is that character trait predicates can be used to evaluate a wide range of quite diverse behaviors. In appraising a person's behavior as generous we are not asserting that it has any single characteristic in common with all other instances of generous behavior; rather, we are indicating that it displays a complex array of characteristics that, taken together, support this evaluation of the action. There will be formal parallels between different instances of generous behavior (e.g., a readiness to meet another's need without counting the cost too closely), but the various "marks" of a generous action can appear in a tremendous variety of different behaviors. There is little prospect of reducing these complex similarities among actions to a fixed set of necessary and sufficient conditions for asserting that an action is generous. Furthermore, character trait predicates will be differently expressed in different actions. The exact meaning of "generosity" in any instance will depend upon the details of the behavior being evaluated. The story about John's behavior must be told if we are to fully appreciate the particular sort of generosity it displays. If there can be an indefinite multiplication of distinct instances of generous behavior, then the particular "values" that generosity can display will vary with tremendous subtlety. A vocabulary of this richness and flexibility clearly holds promise of playing a significant role in theology.

3. DISPOSITIONAL PROPERTIES

The second of my initial three points calls attention to the order of episode-evaluation and person-characterization in the use of character trait predicates. It is John's generous offer (along with other such actions) that leads us to say that John is a generous person. We might well decide that while his offer is generous it is unrepresentative, John being on the whole a rather tight-fisted person. Or we might not make any specific judgment about John himself, but simply appreciate the generosity of his offer. It is not possible, however, to have things the other way around: we cannot sensibly say that John is a generous person, yet be blithely unconcerned at the suggestion that John has never in his life done a generous thing and is not likely to manage one in the future. If we praise John's generosity, we cannot dismiss as irrelevant the request for some instances of generous action.

Once a character trait has been ascribed, we are entitled to expect behavior characterizable by that term in the person's future and to look for such behavior in the person's past. This feature of character trait predicates qualifies them as a special instance of what Gilbert Ryle calls "dispositional properties."[3] This technical notion is not restricted to those prominent emotional or attitudinal characteristics that we ordinarily have in mind when talking about an individual's disposition—that he or she is, for instance, sunny, bright, buoyant, gloomy, dark. These characteristics are good examples of dispositional properties, but they do not exhaust the set of terms that display a "dispositional logic." We ascribe a dispositional property whenever we assert that a "thing, beast or person has a certain capacity, tendency, or propensity, or is subject to a certain liability."[4] Somewhat more precisely, "to possess a dispositional property is not to be in a particular state, or to undergo a particular change; it is to be bound or liable to be in a particular state, or to undergo a particular change, when a particular condition is realized."[5] A predicate can be said to ascribe a disposition in this technical sense if it logically commits us to asserting that the individual to whom it is ascribed is prone to behavior of a certain type on certain occasions.[6]

As Ryle uses the term, then, not only do "moody" and "buoyant" ascribe dispositional properties but so do predicates as diverse as "fragile" and "soluble," "migratory" and "predatory," "conversant in French" and "accomplished as a pianist," "loving" and "generous." Each of these characterizing terms has its sense tied up with a generalization about the behavior of an object (or class of objects) or person. Each directs attention to a pattern in behavior and creates certain expectations for behavior in the future. Each, therefore, seems to be a good example of a dispositional property.

The diversity of these cases is remarkable, however. There are clearly some significant distinctions to be made between these instances of dispositional properties. Both the ascription of generosity to a helpful friend and fragility to a figurine entail that the individual in question is "liable to be in a particular state or undergo a particular change when a particular condition is realized." But there is little prospect of specifying with the same precision in both cases either the behavior to which each is "liable" or the circumstances under which that liability appears.[7] Under the right conditions the fragile object breaks; its fragility consists simply of its liability to this behavior under these conditions. When condition and behavior are identified with sufficient care, the disposition to break can be expressed as a precise *if-then* rule. The disposition to act generously can hardly be given so precise a definition. We have already seen that a trait of character (such as generosity) can be manifested in a tremendous diversity of behaviors. And the circumstances under which generous behavior might occur are correspondingly diverse. There appears to be an inexhaustible variety of actions-in-context that can be appropriately appraised as generous, and it is far from obvious that any simple rule can be stated for the identification of such actions.[8]

Further, in the case of fragility the dispositional property can be ascribed even if an occasion for its exercise never arises. If I warn someone that the glass figurine he holds is fragile, I am not committed to saying that the figurine does frequently break. But if the figurine is struck with great force and does not break, then the claim that it is fragile is (at the very least) called in question. By contrast, a dispositional property such as generosity cannot be ascribed unless it is displayed with a credible frequency in the individual's behavior. But if on any single appropriate occasion the generous person fails to act as we expect, this need not rule out or even seriously call into question the applicability of the dispositional property.[9]

4. THE AMBIGUITY OF "BEHAVIOR"

One might go on to articulate any number of differences among particular dispositional properties. There is one crucial distinction, however, on which I wish to focus. The shattering of a glass figurine is a change of state that the figurine *undergoes* but does not *undertake.* "Making a generous offer," on the other hand, is among those behaviors that we ordinarily would say is undertaken by a person "on purpose," or "intentionally." This brings us to a crucial ambiguity in Ryle's initial definition of dispositional properties. The "behavior" that is called for by the ascription of a dispositional property may be described either as enacted by an agent or as happening to an object. Ryle clearly employs both sorts of description in his account of the behavioral generalizations entailed by dispositional properties. The behavior required by an ascription of vanity, for example, may be provided by speaking at length about oneself, cleaving to the company of the eminent, rejecting criticisms, and so on.[10] The behavior required by an ascription of fragility will be supplied by flying into fragments (rather than, say, denting) when dropped or struck in the required way.[11]

In what follows I will argue that when we ascribe character traits to persons we call attention to patterns in the intentional action of an agent; if we are to appraise behavior by a character trait predicate, we must be able to give a description of that behavior under which we would be willing to say that it was done "on purpose," or "intentionally." Further, I will argue that a description of behavior as intentional action cannot be analyzed exhaustively into a description of behavior as a complex of mere happenings (viz., movements, sounds, changes of state, etc.).[12]

We can begin to give content to this key claim by letting the parrot that Ryle refers to in *The Concept of Mind* (p. 40) perch briefly in our discussion. Suppose that I have been constructing aloud a textbook syllogism, "All men are mortal; Socrates is a man—" and at that point the parrot happens to utter the one set of sounds he has mastered, namely, "Socrates is mortal."[13] We do not appraise this behavior as perceptive or logically acute, nor do we praise the parrot for being quick-witted or for having a good head for arguments. We will not credit an utterance of the set of sounds "Socrates is mortal" with logical acumen even in such an appropriate context unless we are willing to say that it constitutes giving the conclusion to an argument that has been "followed." One might be entertained at the coincidence of the recitation of the premises and the bird's response, and one might enjoy suggesting that the philosophical bird has mastered the argument, but the bird's utterance is nevertheless a paradigmatic instance of behavior that we would not characterize by qualities of intellect precisely because its behavior is best described as "parrotting" the appropriate phrase at an opportune time. The bird, we insist, simply said its piece, enjoying whatever satisfaction a parrot receives from the imitation of human sounds. The parrot's utterance is recognizable as the set of sounds that constitute the English sentence "Socrates is mortal," but we are not prepared to describe the bird's behavior as giving the conclusion to the argument or even as stating that Socrates is mortal, and so we cannot with any seriousness appraise his utterance as logically acute or characterize the bird as brilliant (other than, perhaps, in plumage).

The situation might be different if it were another person, rather than the parrot, who uttered "Socrates is mortal" after I recited the premises from which that conclusion follows. Here we might congratulate the person on his or her logical perceptiveness (particularly if our expectations were not very high). But persons also sometimes simply "parrot" the phrase that in a particular setting can be taken as a correct conclusion, a right answer, a polite response, a clever remark, or the like. Suppose the person who says "Socrates is mortal" had heard the syllogism so many times that he learned the order of the sentences and yet never recognized the logical relations between them (as would the student who simply memorized his lesson in logic). If we knew this about him, we would describe his verbal behavior as "supplying the third sentence in the sequence," and *not* as "making a correct deduction." It is not enough for students to utter "Socrates is mortal" under the appropriate circumstances, even if they intend this as the conclusion to the argument. A further condition must be met: they must have been engaged in an activity that can be described as "following the argument." If their statement is to be appraised as clever or logically perceptive, it must be placed in a wider setting as part of an activity the possible sub-acts of which include noting mistakes, stating the conclusion that one perceives to follow from the premises, and so on.

The characterization of behavior by a character trait predicate depends, therefore, on behavior being taken under a description that is of the appropriate type and that has an appropriate content. The description must be of the type that I will refer to as *intentional action description.* If, for example, a set of sounds is described as a play on words, it might be appropriate to characterize it as clever or witty. But if that same set of sounds is described as a verbal slip, then it cannot be characterized as witty, even if it is amusing. Ordinarily, if a person's statement is properly described as a play on words, it is appropriate to say, and would be quite odd to deny, that he uttered it *as* a play on words, with that intention. On the other hand, if his statement is correctly described as a verbal slip it is ordinarily inappropriate to say that he uttered it *as* a verbal slip, with the intention of making a verbal mistake (for in that case his utterance is not a mistake at all). If behavior is to be characterized by a trait of character term, it must be taken under a description of the same type as "a play on words" (i.e., a description that could appropriately be made the object of a sentence of the form, "He intended . . . ."). A description of behavior simply as a set of sounds, movements, or changing relations of objects provides no basis for appraisal by character trait predicates.

In saying that these predicates appraise behavior taken as the intentional action of an agent, I am not saying that the agent must have intended to display the character trait that is ascribed to him. Especially when the appraisal is negative, the agent is not likely to have set out to be characterized in this way. Neither is the agent in any privileged position with regard to the appraisal of his own behavior. An individual will usually not be aware of most of the appraisals that might be made of his intentional actions. Often others will be able to make a more perceptive judgment than can the agent himself.[14] But if an individual has no intention in his behavior (i.e., if it cannot be described as intentional action), then his behavior cannot be appraised by character trait predicates at all. An agent need not intend that his behavior be generous in order that it be appraised as generous. But if his behavior is to be judged generous, he must undertake it as a project the description of which (both in intention and execution) renders it subject to that appraisal.

Not only must the description of behavior be of the appropriate type, it must have a content appropriate to the particular character trait being ascribed. Obviously no single predicate can be applied to behavior under every conceivable intentional action description. Behavior indicative of staggering drunkenness will be subject to a different appraisal when described as "trying to find where he parked the car" than when described as "clowning for some friends." It will be correct to ascribe a particular character trait predicate only if the behavior so characterized falls within a certain range of intentional action descriptions. We have already noted that this range of appraisable actions cannot be fixed with precision and may well embrace a great variety of specific instances. A parent may be patient in supervising his child's play, a philosopher patient in constructing his argument, a general patient in conducting a military campaign. In each instance the actions involved may display similar qualities of forbearance, sustained attention, and resistance to the temptation of a quick solution. Yet these actions belong to widely different areas of life and express quite diverse particular intentions.

We might pause here for a moment and take our bearings. If my argument so far is sound, then there is a necessary logical relation between, say, being a generous person and performing generous actions. In using our language of character traits to describe a person's distinctive identity we are calling attention to patterns in the way he conducts his life as an agent of intentional actions. This clearly locates the conceptual hinge on which will turn any talk of God in personal categories, for example, as being wise, just, and loving. This language requires that we think of God as an agent of intentional actions. My central task here is to examine the concepts of intentional action and agency and to explore the use of these concepts in thinking about God. In the following two sections of this chapter, I will joust briefly with views that try to avoid giving the concept of intentional action any fundamental role in understanding persons. The argument of these sections provides philosophical backing for my claim that a distinction between intentional action and mere happening is built into the language we use in describing persons. I will sum up the results of this discussion in the concluding section of this chapter and turn to the concept of intentional action in Chapter 2.

5. RYLE ON INTENTIONAL ACTION

Traits of character appraise behavior not merely as a set of events that happen to take place, but as the intentional action of an agent. But is the distinction between intentional action and happening irreducible? One might argue that any description of behavior as intentional action can be analyzed into a complex set of dispositions to certain occurrences (i.e., movements, utterances, etc.) in certain circumstances. Ryle's discussion of "heeding," "trying," and "intending" at least raises this possibility, though he does not carry it through consistently. He asks about the "special character" that distinguishes an attentive or purposeful action from an overtly identical behavior performed absent-mindedly or inadvertently.[15] The difference, he insists, must consist "either in the concomitant occurrence of some internal actions and reactions, detectable only by the performer, or else in the satisfaction by the overt performances of different open hypothetical statements."[16] The difference between a clever remark and a verbal slip that are overtly identical lies either in the fact that the clever remark is the effect of a mental episode distinct from the overt utterance or else in the different behavioral expectations established by these two descriptions. Since Ryle concludes that the first proposal is absurd, we are left with the second.

Ryle acknowledges that neither of these options seems acceptable as it stands, but in spite of his disdain for those who are "spellbound by dichotomies," he never alters this dichotomy in any fundamental way. Rather he points out that in referring to an individual as heeding what he is doing, we are not *only* saying that certain behavioral generalizations apply to him, but we are also saying that his present activity is an instance of the behavior called for by those generalizations. A "mongrel-categorical" or "semi-hypothetical" statement of this kind does not refer us "behind the scenes" to the operations of an agent of behavior.[17] Rather, it places the particular behavior in the wider setting of some set of regularities, as in the case of referring to a bird's progress south as "migrating." Hence, "being interested in reading [a] book is not doing or undergoing two things, such that the interest is the cause of the reading. The interest explains the reading in the same general way, though not the same specific way, as the migrating explains the flying south."[18] Here the original dichotomy stands unmodified.

Ryle's proposal that we offer a dispositional analysis of statements about heeding, trying, and intending is correct as a point about the entailment patterns of such statements but unilluminating as an answer to the question he has raised about the "special character" of attentive and intentional behaviors. It is correct to say that the statement "John is trying to keep the deer out of his cornfield" entails that John does from time to time take actions that can appropriately be described, whatever more specific descriptions might be given, as "trying to keep the deer out of his cornfield."[19] That is hardly a surprising philosophical discovery. Nor is it a particularly useful observation in thinking through the question Ryle has raised about the distinction between "trying to do X" and "just happening to do X." Ryle's dispositional account of intending is ambiguous with regard to precisely the distinction it is supposed to illuminate. We are left asking again whether the "behavior" that is called for by a description of behavior as performed "on purpose" is to be taken as intentional action or mere happening. If "behavior" in these generalizations includes intentional action, then Ryle's dispositional analysis sheds no light on the notion of "intending." We do learn something from this analysis about the logical structure of descriptions of behavior as intentional action, namely, intentional action descriptions are knitted together in a complex pattern of entailments. But the notion of intentional action is not illuminated by saying that if we describe a behavior as intentional we are logically committed to saying that certain other intentional actions are likely to be performed as well. The initial question simply arises again.

Ryle would be giving a genuine answer to his question, however, if he were suggesting that talk of an agent's intention can be understood in terms of sets of hypothetical generalizations correlating overt circumstances with behavior taken simply as happening. Ryle could not be accused of begging his own question if he were claiming that statements about intention can be translated exhaustively into statements about movements of bodies, utterances of sounds, and so on, under certain conditions. This would leave him with a thoroughly behaviorist account of statements describing human behavior as purposive. There would then be no irreducible difference between action and happening. Talk of a person's intentions would be equivalent to assertion of certain complex generalizations about what will happen under certain circumstances.

But Ryle does not carry through a consistent behaviorist analysis; rather, he usually includes intentional actions in the behavioral dispositions that express the content of references to trying or intending.[20] And at certain points he explicitly and quite articulately rejects a behaviorism to which he elsewhere appears congenial.[21] But neither does Ryle develop a nonbehaviorist account of intentional action. His insistence that mind-body dualism and dispositional analysis are exhaustive alternatives suggests the reason: he tends to see all talk of the agent's purposive enactment of behavior as indebted to the mind-body dualism he attacks throughout *The Concept of Mind.* He is not alive to the possibility of speaking of an agent's conscious regulation of his behavior without treating such activity as the regulation of behavior by consciousness (mind). As a result, he leans toward (without ever consistently adopting) a strictly behaviorist account of descriptions of behavior as intentional action.[22]

6. PHILOSOPHICAL BEHAVIORISM AND INTENTIONAL ACTION

Can the thoroughgoing behaviorism that Ryle avoids be worked out in a convincing way? Such a behaviorism would refuse to draw any irreducible distinction between action and happening. All statements about what persons intend would be resolved into sets of statements about overt occurrences.

The difficulties facing such a proposal appear to be insurmountable. We do ordinarily say of a person who is engaged, for example, in the intentional activity of working out a philosophical argument that *if* someone were to point out a mistake, *then* he or she would revise the argument to eliminate it. But for at least two reasons this informal derivation of a hypothetical proposition from an intentional-action description does not help the behaviorist. First, and most obviously, the behavior noted in the hypothetical proposition is itself an intentional action, and, as noted above, the behaviorist must eliminate all reference to intentional action. Descriptions of behavior as intentional action must be reexpressed strictly in terms of hypothetical propositions correlating observable circumstance with behavior *qua* happening. Whatever plausibility behaviorism may have derives at least in part from its failure thoroughly to rid itself (in its systematic language) of familiar ways of describing behavior that imply or suggest purposiveness. Second, it is not enough for the behaviorist to note certain behaviors that, in the appropriate circumstances, characteristically identify a performance as falling under a particular intentional action description. If a set of hypothetical propositions are to express the *meaning* of an intentional action description, then they must be entailed by that description. It must be self-contradictory to insist upon the correctness of an intentional-action description if any one of these hypothetical propositions should fail to apply.

At this point the enormous implausibility of this behaviorism emerges. It is not at all clear that the occurrence of some specific set of movements, sounds, and so on in some specific set of circumstances is entailed by each intentional-action description. In most instances there is a wide range of different ways of performing an intentional action that do not change its description. A philosopher constructing an argument need not do so sitting at his desk and making marks on paper. He may construct his argument verbally in conversation, or silently "in his head," or operatically in his morning shower. In each case his activity can be described as "constructing an argument." Perhaps these are not the sorts of behaviors that will define "constructing an argument"; instead, we should refer to certain distinctive patterns in the activity of associating symbols, however and wherever this is done. But is it plausible to suggest that these tremendously diverse patterns of symbol association could in principle yield some set of behavioral generalizations that must apply to any individual who is constructing an argument? It seems very unlikely that a determinate set of *if-then* correlations between particular circumstances and observable behaviors (in the narrow sense) constitutes the content of this or any other intentional-action description.

If behaviorists have difficulty handling the diversity of behaviors that can be brought under a single intentional-action description, they will also have difficulty handling diverse intentional-action descriptions of identical behaviors. Ryle mentions the case of a performance at the piano that might be taken either as an original interpretation or as a parody of a rival pianist's style.[23] What account might behaviorists give of the difference in these descriptions? They would have to argue that if these descriptions are in fact to differ in meaning, then each must entail at least one circumstance-behavior correlation that differs from those entailed by the other. There must, that is, be some circumstances under which observable behavior (in the narrow sense) would decisively differentiate between "parodying" and "seriously interpreting." But it appears impossible to identify any such circumstance-behavior generalizations. There are a variety of ways in which we might tell whether one is doing a parody or offering a serious interpretation: the performer may exaggerate certain quirks of keyboard style, overdo characteristic patterns of musical interpretation, chuckle privately about the performance, and so on. But any one of these identifying marks may be absent without our being forced to conclude that the performance is a serious interpretation. It is hard to imagine any single behavioral pattern that *must* occur in a given circumstance if a performance is to be meaningfully described as a parody. It *may* be correct to say that a performance cannot be a parody, even though the performer intends it as such, unless it somehow shows itself to be a parody. That is, the pianist's attempt at parody will not succeed unless it gives itself away, though it may do so with the most artful subtlety. But the particular behavioral cues that allow us to decide whether the performance is a parody or a serious interpretation are not entailed by these action descriptions, and so cannot provide the difference in meaning between them.

A behaviorist might reply that these objections cast his views in too rigid a form. He might grant the implausibility of suggesting that action descriptions are equivalent to sets of *if-then* generalizations about circumstances and behavior. The distinctive behavioral patterns to which we call attention in typical action descriptions are too complex to be given so simple and binding a form. Rather, in describing behavior as a particular intentional action, we point out a variegated pattern of probabilities for how that behavior will unfold. The choice of a particular action description asserts that behavior is more likely to develop in one way rather than another under any given set of circumstances. These probable developments cannot be expressed as law-like *if-then* hypotheticals. They take a form more like "If 'x,' then more likely than not 'y'." An ambiguous case, such as that of the pianist's performance, can now be handled more readily. There may simply be no single circumstance-behavior generalization that decisively differentiates between the two action descriptions. The difference in meaning between the rival descriptions consists in the complex pattern of behavioral probabilities entailed by each of them.

This defense of behaviorism must insist that these *if-then likely* correlations do not need to be explained or resolved into high-probability *if-then* correlations; rather, low-probability correlations are simply "found in the data." If one refuses, however, to treat low-probability correlations as merely provisional, then explanations of familiar human behavior, which for psychologically uncomplicated inquiries are complete, would not be complete and could not be completed. A question such as "Why did John attend that concert?" could receive an answer no more specific than "It was likely that he would." For if we say "He is a music lover," all we have done is to place his behavior in the setting of low-probability correlations of certain observable circumstances (e.g., the frequency of concerts, the availability of new recordings, etc.) and certain behaviors. This amounts simply to saying, "Well, if there is a concert, John is likely to attend." If one persists in the inquiry, there is nothing any more illuminating that can be said. A statement such as "A Mozart piano concerto was on the program, and John loves Mozart's music" does nothing more than point to another *if-then likely* correlation that, *ex hypothesi,* cannot itself be given a more precise expression in terms of high-probability *if-then* correlations.

This is not the end of the behaviorist's problems. Even if we suppose it possible in principle to translate descriptions of behavior as intentional action into exhaustive sets of hypothetical propositions about observable occurrences, the resulting behaviorism has some peculiar implications. Note, for example, that we often ask persons to tell us what they are doing. If there is no reason to call the agent's honesty in question, and if we are not probing for a psychologically profound analysis, we usually take the question to be settled by the agent's response. The behaviorist clearly cannot make sense of this procedure. First-person statements of the form "I am 'x-ing' " cannot be taken by the behaviorist as avowals of intention that can settle the issue between alternative action descriptions when behavioral information is insufficient. Such statements must be generalizations about behavior no different in status than characterizations by an observer. If behavior is ambiguous with regard to alternative action descriptions for the third-person observer, it will be ambiguous for the first-person subject of the description as well.

Here is one of the more ironic results of the behaviorist's analysis of intentional-action descriptions: if the first-person basis of a description of intention can be no different than that of the third-person observer, then I can know my own intentions only by observing my behavior. In difficult cases I will have to "wait and see what I do next" before making a judgment about the correct description of what I intend. And in persistently ambiguous cases the only intellectually responsible attitude for me to adopt will be a complete suspension of judgment about what I am trying to do.

CONCLUSION

If behaviorism fails, we are left with an irreducible distinction between descriptions of behavior as intentional action and descriptions of behavior as merely a complex of overt movements, utterances, and so on. It is the task of the next chapter to develop the concept of intentional action at greater length. But we should pause here and note the results of the discussion to date.

The language we use in characterizing persons as distinctive individuals displays a dispositional logic—that is, it calls attention to patterns in a person's behavior across time. The central concern of my argument thus far has been to claim that the behavior to which we call attention in ascribing traits of character must be intentional action. When we describe someone as wise or generous, we note certain persistent characteristics of the way that person conducts his life, for example, the content of the projects he conceives, the pattern of his deliberation and decision, the style of his performances, the character of his accomplishments. These patterns of action may be quite complex and the judgments involved in appraising them very difficult. This is part of the reason we often explain what we mean in ascribing a character trait by telling a story about the person's behavior in a particular situation. We say, in effect, "When I say that John is generous, I mean that you can look for behavior of this sort in circumstances of this kind." This suggestion, however, cannot be fixed in the frozen simplicity of a "law-like hypothetical proposition."[24] Rather, we signal or typify John's distinctive sort of generosity in the episode we narrate. The quality that we wish to point out in this person may appear in a wide range of particular behaviors. We will continue to learn something about the special way in which John is generous as we see him confront novel situations. And we may learn something new from this about the ways in which a person can be generous.

Character trait predicates, then, constitute a vocabulary of great flexibility and richness that is keyed to the identification of significant continuities in intentional action. What we ordinarily refer to as character appears in the complexly interwoven patterns of a person's purposive activity. When we characterize an individual as the bearer of a distinctive personal identity, we necessarily treat him as an agent of intentional actions.

This has obvious and important implications with regard to talk of God. If we are to say that God is loving or just, we must be prepared to point to actions in which his love and justice are displayed. Love and justice will be attributes of God only if these terms are appropriate appraisals of his actions. The meaning of these attributes will be tied logically to the account that we give of what God has done and is doing. The particular way in which God is loving or just will appear in the story we tell about God's activity in relation to his creation. And even more dramatically than with other agents, this story-telling will not fully capture the qualities that we attribute to God, but will at most typify them.

All of this holds some important clues for rethinking traditional doctrines of the "moral perfections" of God, but the general point that I want to underscore at this stage of the discussion is that God will bear these personal attributes as an agent whose identity is made manifest in action. This can be given more general expression by saying that if God is to be a *personal* being, then he must be an agent of intentional actions. The concepts "personal" and "nonpersonal" are quite slippery. The distinction they identify is surely a distinction of degree, and so resists precise definition; the rough contours of the distinction show themselves, however, in the familiar sets of predicates that we readily ascribe to subjects that we would be willing to call "personal" but withhold from subjects that we would call "nonpersonal." Character trait predicates clearly constitute a prominent set of such terms. Indeed, it would appear that unless a fairly rich selection of such predicates can be ascribed to a subject, that subject cannot be considered personal. But in this case the necessary conditions for the use of character trait predicates will also be necessary conditions for talk of any subject as personal (viz., that subject must be an agent).

This sets the central question for the rest of my study: How might we systematically employ the language of personal agency in thinking about God? What difficulties must be faced by any attempt to conceive of God as one who acts?

The first step toward answering these questions must be a careful consideration of the concept of intentional action. I have argued that descriptions of behavior as intentional action are not reducible to descriptions of behavior as mere happening. By taking a more detailed look at this distinction we can bring into view the central issues at stake in talk of personal agency.

CHAPTER 2

Intentional Action

1. THE AGENT'S DISPOSITION TO ACT

If we reject the behaviorist's analysis of action, we need not deny that intentional-action descriptions create expectations about how behavior will unfold in future circumstances. In ascribing an intention we do indeed ascribe a "disposition." When we say that an individual intends an action A, we must be willing to say that he is ready to act in ways that he believes will satisfy the description of A when there is an appropriate occasion to do so. If an individual professes to intend an action A and does not display, on an appropriate occasion, behavior that can be taken as an attempt to perform A, then we suppose that he did not recognize the occasion as appropriate, that something happened that made it impossible for him to enact his intention, that his intention was more complex than we had known (e.g., that it was conditional upon some situational factor of which we were unaware), or that he changed his mind. Unless an explanation of this sort can be offered, it is not simply untrue but rather nonsensical to say that an agent intended to perform action A when one knows that he did not even try to perform that action.

If my objections to behaviorism are convincing, however, the behavioral disposition entailed by an intentional-action description will not be simply a statistical probability that certain movements will take place in certain circumstances; rather, "disposition" will have an irreducibly agential sense. When we describe behavior as intentional action we say that the agent is directing his behavior in accord with the aim, or purpose, that the description of his action articulates: the agent is disposed, we could say, to undertake actions that might reasonably be expected to realize his purposes. Two things of central importance are involved here: a description of behavior as intentional action (1) calls attention to the agent's purpose, or aim, in his movements, utterances, and so forth, and (2) credits him with regulating his behavior in accord with that purpose. These two features of talk of intentional action are inextricably bound together. In offering an intentional-action description of an agent's behavior, we suppose not only that the agent intends behavior of that description but also that he brings about that behavior. The discussion that follows develops these two points, beginning with the notion of an agent's intention in action.

2. INTENTION IN ACTION

An agent's aim in his action will always be, most concretely and immediately, to carry through some pattern of performance, or "project." The various projects that an agent enacts will vary in the degree of articulation that precedes action. Deliberate selection from among well-defined options usually provides the paradigmatic example of intentional action, but much of a human being's life is characterized by intentional activity that is less self-conscious and articulated than this. We are constantly recognizing possibilities for action and discriminating among them informally. Most of the possible projects we contemplate are initially undetailed, leaving open specifically how the action will be performed, such as taking a walk (around this block or that? across the fields or down the road?), murdering Julius Caesar (now or later? with conspirators or alone? in the Senate or in the baths?), or respecting the best interests of others (as a general policy to be specified in particular situations). We do not always (or even very often) plot out the detail of an action in advance of undertaking it. Instead we "play it by ear," filling in the specifics of a project as we carry it through under a general description. As we opt for particular ways of carrying through an undetailed project, we may modify the character of that undertaking. Our actions often develop out of one another as our activity churns up new possibilities.

This complex process of recognizing and selectively pursuing lines of action occasionally becomes explicit deliberation between well-developed alternatives. But it need not take this more articulated form in order to count as intentional action. Indeed, an agent who is acting intentionally may not be able to communicate in words the precise details of what he is trying to do. An artist, for example, may describe in general terms the outcome he is seeking on the canvas, yet be unable to say precisely how he proceeds or exactly what final arrangement of colors, spaces, textures, and so forth he intends.[1] He may know when he has achieved what he wants, and he may know how to go about achieving it, and yet he may not be able to say to his own or another's satisfaction what he has achieved or how he has arrived at it. The perceptive art critic may do a better job here. Whether easily verbalized or not, however, it is precisely in this process of recognizing, assessing, and critically pursuing possibilities for action that skills are exercised and that traits of character are displayed.

I have suggested that an agent's intention in action will be to carry through some pattern of performance, or project, that he has set for himself. The reason for stating the matter this way can be seen by considering the senses in which an agent might be said to seek a particular end, or outcome, in his action. An agent will always intend an outcome of action in the sense of intending that his actual performance successfully carry through the general project he has undertaken. We will call this intended project the "outcome_1" that the agent seeks to realize in his action. Often the pattern of action one envisions will, under one description A_1 (e.g., "throwing a basketball," "ringing a bell"), be ordered to some further action of description A_2 that is brought about by the performance of A_1 (e.g., "making a basket," "calling people to dinner").[2] We will call A_2 the "outcome_2" of A_1. One will not in every case intend an outcome_2 of action. An agent may undertake behavior of the description "ringing the bell" without the further intention of "calling people to dinner," or he may "call people to dinner" with the further intention of "keeping people on schedule." Behavior under any one of these descriptions is intentional whether or not it is undertaken in order to satisfy some further project description. As long as there is at least one action description that an agent seeks to satisfy as the outcome_1 of his behavior, his behavior (taken under that description) is intentional.

This point can perhaps be made more clearly by distinguishing several interrelated mistakes that might be made in stating a criterion for intentional action. We can begin with two complementary proposals. First, one might say that in order for any behavior to be intentional it must be the $outcome_2$ sought by action under another description. If, that is, a behavior of description A_n is to count as intentional, it must be the further intention ($outcome_2$) with which behavior under some other description A_{n-1} is undertaken. Second, one might say that in order for any behavior to count as intentional, it must be instrumental to the realization of some further purpose ($outcome_2$). If, that is, a behavior of description A_n is to count as intentional, it must be undertaken as the means of generating action under some further description A_{n+1} as its $outcome_2$.

Many of the things we do fit one or both of these descriptions. Many actions do have an instrumental substructure—that is, they are the $outcome_2$ of action under another description (e.g., "ringing the bell" may be the $outcome_2$ of "pulling a rope"). And many of our actions are, under one description, instrumental to carrying through action under another description (as when I "ring the bell" in order to "call people to dinner"). But either of these patterns, if taken as the sole model for a general account of intentional behavior, will produce an infinite regress.

If we adopt the first criterion, then any behavior will be an intentional action A_n only if it is the intended $outcome_2$ of some other behavior A_{n-1}. A_{n-1} cannot be inadvertent or automatic (i.e., a subintentional occurrence), for then it would make no sense to speak of A_n as a further action ($outcome_2$) that A_{n-1} intended. Hence, A_{n-1} must itself be an intentional action, and so must be the $outcome_2$ of some other behavior A_{n-2}. But again, A_{n-2} must be intentional and so must be the outcome of A_{n-3}, which itself must be the $outcome_2$ of A_{n-4}, and so on, *ad infinitum.*

If we adopt the second criterion, then any behavior will be an intentional action A_n only if it is intended to bring about some action A_{n+1}. But it would make no sense to say that while A_n is intentional, the $outcome_2$ sought by A_n is not. So A_{n+1} must itself be an intentional action. But if all intentional actions are by definition undertaken in order to realize some further $outcome_2$, then A_{n+1} must itself be intended to generate the further action A_{n+2}. A_{n+2} must also be intentional, however, and so must intend a further action A_{n+3}, and so on, *ad infinitum*.

These difficulties are only compounded if we conjoin the two criteria, for in that case any behavior will be an intentional action

A_n only if it is *both* the outcome$_2$ of action under another description A_{n-1} *and* is intended to generate some further action A_{n+1}. If we deny that either A_{n-1} or A_{n+1} is an intentional action, then we face the same absurdities noted above, namely, that it makes no sense to say that A_n is the outcome$_2$ intended by a subintentional occurrence; nor does it make sense to say that the outcome$_2$ that A_n intends is a subintentional occurrence. But if A_{n-1} and A_{n+1} are both intentional actions, then a regress is generated in both directions at once. A_{n-1} will be intentional only if it is the outcome$_2$ of action under another description A_{n-2}, which is the outcome$_2$ of A_{n-3}, and so on. A_{n+1} will be intentional only if intended to generate a further action A_{n+2}, which intended to generate A_{n+3}, and so on.

Perhaps the way out of these difficulties lies neither in taking each criterion singly nor in conjoining them, but rather in disjoining them. We then say that any behavior that is an intentional action A_n is so *either* by virtue of being undertaken as the means of generating some further action A_{n+1} as its outcome$_2$ *or* by virtue of being the outcome$_2$ for the sake of which action was undertaken under another description A_{n-1}. This allows that the intentional action A_n may be the outcome$_2$ of some other action A_{n-1} without being intended to generate any further action under another description A_{n+1}. And this allows that the intentional action A_{n-1} might be intended to bring about the further action A_n without A_{n-1} itself being the outcome$_2$ of action under another description A_{n-2}. Hence, regress is stopped in both directions.

It is important to note, however, that this criterion requires that every intentional action (A_n) have action under another description either as its antecedent (A_{n-1}) or as its intended outcome (A_{n+1}). Every intentional action will be part of an "instrumental action sequence" of performing one action in order to generate a further action. This requirement rules out a large number of behaviors that we ordinarily want to allow as intentional actions. I may, for example, raise my hand with no intention beyond the raising of the hand and without (as I will argue later) having to perform an intentional action of any other description as the condition for bringing it about that I raise my hand. In this case we want to say *both* that my behavior is an intentional action *and* that it does not belong to an instrumental action sequence—that it is neither the outcome$_2$ of action under another description nor the means of generating action under some further description. There is no reason to exclude from the category of intentional actions, as a matter of definition, all behaviors *not* belonging to an instrumental action sequence. It should be possible to undertake behavior of a particular description *on purpose* without undertaking that behavior *for a purpose* (i.e., for a further purpose). The concept of intentional action must be cut loose from any essential relation to the instrumental action sequence "doing A_1 in order to do A_2."

What is being said, then, in describing an agent's behavior as performed "on purpose," or "intentionally"? An agent's behavior is intentional if he seeks an outcome_1 (i.e., the satisfaction of some action description A_n in his performance) whether or not he intends behavior of a further description A_{n+1} as the outcome_2 of A_n, and whether or not A_n is itself an outcome_2 of behavior under another description A_{n-1}. Further, if infinite regress is to be prevented, every instrumental action sequence must (1) involve a sub-action that is intentional but is not the outcome_2 of any other intentional action and (2) involve a sub-action that is intentional but is not taken as a means of producing action under any further description as its outcome_2. Finally, if we allow that some actions do *not* belong to an instrumental sequence, then there will be some instances in which action under a *single* description satisfies *both* of these requirements.

Let us see how these formal remarks can be applied to some concrete examples. Note, for example, the action that is described by "ringing the bell." This action does have a complex intentional substructure. I may have to pull a rope in order to ring the bell and move my body in certain ways in order to pull the rope. I might even, a dualist could argue, need to perform certain mental acts of volition in order to move my body in the appropriate ways. At some point, however, this instrumental regress must come to an end in an action that I do, *not* by doing anything else, but simply by undertaking it.[3] This will be a "basic," or "intentionally simple," action—that is, an action that is intentional but that is not the outcome_2 of any other intentional action.[4] We will return to the notion of basic actions in section 2 of Chapter 5.

It is important to note that when a basic action is subsumed under a more extensive project, it may not be explicitly treated as a distinctive intentional unit. When an action has an analyzable intentional substructure, I do not focus my attention upon every identifiable sub-act as an explicit project. The focus of my attention will usually be determined by the special relevance of any particular detail of action to the overall effect that I seek, as, for example, when the rope must be pulled with just the correct force and rhythm if the bell is to sound at all: if no special obstacle is encountered, my attention may be focused on the intended effect and "pass over" the detail of behavior involved in producing that effect. Hence, an action may have a complex intentional structure without that complexity being represented in the detail of an agent's conscious articulation of his project.

Though I perform certain movements in order to pull the rope, and pull the rope in order to ring the bell, I may have no intention in ringing the bell beyond the successful execution of the behavior so described. We have seen, however, that behavior need not be instrumental to some further aim in order to be purposive; it is necessary only that the behavior be performed on purpose, or intentionally—that is, it is necessary only that "ringing the bell" be a correct description of the project that I have undertaken. An agent who rings the bell just for the fun of it has no aim in his behavior beyond its execution under the description "ringing the bell." His action of ringing the bell is performed *on* purpose but not *for* a purpose, as the means of producing action under some further description as its outcome$_2$.

One might, of course, have any of a number of further intentions in ringing the bell. When there is some further intention that runs beyond one's immediate action under a narrower description, we often take that wider intention as an overall description of the action the person is engaged in. One may, for example, ring the bell in order to call people to dinner. In that case we would appropriately describe one's action either as "ringing the bell" or as "calling people to dinner." The latter of these two descriptions gives us a more complete picture of what the agent is doing than does the former.[5] It is possible, as well, that the agent might have further intentions in calling people to dinner; he might, for instance, intend to keep people on a proper schedule or to safeguard their health through correct eating habits. It is interesting to note, however, that not every description that might correctly be given of what an agent intends in his behavior will be accepted as a description of the action he is performing. We might well hesitate to describe the bell ringer's behavior as "safeguarding people's health," except perhaps to poke fun at the scope and seriousness of his broader intentions in this rather mundane task. When the risk of failure is high, or when the action an agent intends is described in terms of its successful execution (e.g., "fixing my car"), or when the connection between one's action and its intended outcome is tenuous (as in the case of the bell ringer concerned with the diners' health), then we are apt to add "trying . . ." to the description we give of his action (e.g., "He is trying to run a four minute mile").

If an agent has no further purpose in his behavior beyond its performance under a particular description, then an interesting shift takes place in the type of explanation given for his action. Suppose someone asks, "Why are you pulling on that rope?" The question treats "pulling the rope" as an intentional action in need of explanation. If in response the agent points out the subordination of "pulling the rope" to "ringing the bell," and if he has no further purpose to which ringing the bell is subordinate, then explanation in terms of agent intention will come to an end at that point. If we ask the agent *why* he acts as he does, we will no longer be asking "With what purpose do you act?" but rather "Why do you act with that purpose?" Explanation will now proceed by pointing to the motivational background for undertaking an action of that description. At some point in any explanation of intentional action, purposive explanation will either come to an end or reach a level of generality so far removed from the particular action in question that the explanation is no longer useful or illuminating.

In short, when an agent initiates behavior under some general action description in an effort to carry through a project defined by that description, his behavior is intentional whether or not it has a complex intentional substructure or envisions some further $outcome_2$ for the sake of which it is undertaken. Many of our actions will be intended as the further $outcome_2$ that is sought in acting under another description. And many of our actions will be intended to bring about action under some further description as their $outcome_2$. But all of our actions will be intended as the satisfaction of an action description that is adopted as the norm for our performance.

3. UNINTENTIONAL ACTION

I have been arguing that when we describe an agent's intentional action we describe his behavior in terms of a project that he has set for himself. As we have just seen, there may be correct descriptions of what an agent intends that are not appropriate as descriptions of his action. We must now note that there will be, as well, correct descriptions of an agent's action that are not descriptions of what he intends. If a behavior description does not capture what an individual has set out to do, then it is not a description of the intentional action he has undertaken, even though it may be an accurate account of what he actually has accomplished.

Agents sometimes make mistakes (e.g., I might decide to dispose of *my* donkey but gun down *your* donkey, having "mistaken" him for mine). And agents sometimes do things "by accident" (e.g., I might gun down your donkey when he suddenly steps in front of mine).[6] In either case, a description of what the agent has done is not a description of what he intends, since he fails to achieve what he intends.

Apart from mistakes and accidents, and even when we accomplish what we intend, our behavior is continually open to descriptions that correctly state what we *do* though they differ from the description under which we *intentionally act* and though we may be unaware that they describe our behavior. This perhaps is inevitable. For an agent will intend his behavior under only a limited selection of the descriptions that might be given of it. Our bell ringer, for example, may have no intention in his action beyond the ringing of the bell. It may nonetheless be true that by ringing the bell he calls people to dinner. When confronted by irate diners assembled for a meal that is not yet prepared, the bell ringer will insist that he did not call them to dinner "on purpose." "Calling people to dinner" describes what he did, but not what he intended to do.

The plausibility of his claim will be greatly diminished, of course, if it turns out that he knew or suspected that ringing the bell was the signal for dinner. If he did know this, it would hardly calm his accusers to be told that all he intended was to ring the bell. One is usually held responsible to take into consideration the probable consequences of a contemplated action. If an agent is aware of inevitable consequences of his action, and particularly if those consequences are of importance to other persons, then his claim *not* to have brought about those consequences "on purpose" may well be dismissed as morally dishonest.

This points to the complexity of questions about which descriptions of an agent's action should be taken as descriptions of his intention. One might suggest that in undertaking an action A in circumstance C one must intend whatever is unavoidably involved in carrying through A in C.[7] But the notion of "whatever is unavoidably involved in carrying through A" is ambiguous. The phrase might or might not include the following:

1. whatever is believed to be a necessary condition in circumstance C for bringing about A (e.g., pulling the rope in order to ring the bell);
2. whatever results from or is concomitantly brought about by doing A (e.g., calling people to dinner by ringing the bell, breaking the bell, frightening the pigeons);
3. whatever I do under descriptions of my behavior yielded by true redescriptions of the direct and indirect objects of my action (e.g., if "ringing the bell" describes my intentional action, my behavior might be redescribed as "ringing a bell that has not sounded since the death of Robert E. Lee"; if "making Jones chairman of the transportation committee" describes my intentional action, my behavior might be redescribed as "making a drunk the chairman of the body that oversees highway safety").

Now, we might well say that in undertaking action A one intends "whatever is involved in carrying through A" in the first of the above senses of that phrase. With some appropriate qualifications, one could argue plausibly that in acting intentionally one intends, even if one does not attend to, the detail of the project. But it seems clear that there will be many cases in which one does not intend "whatever is involved in carrying through action A" in either of the other two senses. One might, of course, undertake a particular action in a particular way precisely because that action can be redescribed in ways that are appealing or because performing that action will have certain desirable consequences. Though these redescriptions and consequences are incidental to one's primary aim, we may wish to speak of them as secondary intentions that are of subordinate importance to the agent. Equally, however, one might undertake action *in spite of* these possible redescriptions and consequences. In that case, these "by-products" of the action might not enter into a description of what the agent intends, and we would not say that the agent is *trying* to perform the behavior of these descriptions. If it were in fact possible to perform the action he intends without his behavior bearing these consequences, he could do so without changing his intention. These unavoidable (though sometimes acknowledged) concomitants of intentional action may or may not be termed "intentional" depending upon the interests of an inquiry about them and the circumstances of the action.

An agent's own description of his project will obviously play a central role in determining our answer to these questions about his intention in action. If behavior is to count as intentional action, it must be taken under a description that identifies not simply what the agent might be said to have done, but what he undertook. We must at least note, however, that there may be cases in which we say that an agent is confused about his aims in action or even unaware of them. Psychoanalytic references to subconscious motives, interests, and aims raise a host of difficult questions that run beyond the immediate interests of this essay. For our purposes, references to aims of which the agent is unaware raise a question about the concept of intentional action. Must (logically) an agent know what he intends? Must any description of his intentional action be a description that, presuming that the meaning of the description is clear, the agent would recognize and accept without hesitation?

If an agent does not know he has performed behavior of a particular description, we very often take this as sufficient grounds for saying that he did not perform that behavior intentionally. This is the case, for example, with most of the appropriate redescriptions of an agent's behavior of which the agent is unaware. The action of the politician who makes Jones chairman of the transportation committee, for instance, may be redescribed as "making a drunk the chairman of the committee that oversees highway safety," but this cannot be taken as a description of the politician's intention unless he knew of his appointee's weakness for Scotch whisky. It may also be the case that the politician's action can be redescribed as "filling his administration with individuals he can easily dominate," and in this instance the politician may himself acknowledge at a later date that this correctly describes his intention, though at the time of making his appointments he was unaware of it. How is this situation to be understood?

It will help here to recall two points that we have already made about intentional action. First, many of our actions are not only performed *on* purpose, but also *for* a purpose. That is, many of the intentional actions ascribed to an agent can be placed in the context of some broader intention to which the particular action in question is relevant. This move from a particular intentional action to a broader project in which it has a place is one of the most common techniques we use in explaining one another's actions. The longer-term intentional patterns (the projects of broader scope) in which a particular action may have a place can be unarticulated and quite complex. I noted earlier that much (and perhaps most) of our recognition and discrimination among options for action does not become articulate planning and deliberate decision. We often do not reflect extensively upon why we undertake one action rather than another. We do not always (or even very often) examine the long-range intentions and broader patterns of preference that provide the context for interest in this action here and now. When we do try to understand our particular actions in a broader explanatory context, the results are occasionally startling. We may discover patterns of action of which we had been unaware; we may come to link actions together that we had not previously seen as connected. A particular action will then be recognized as belonging to a broader project, though we did not perform that action with any clear awareness of acting for this further purpose. We may, in short, come to say both that an action was undertaken for a further purpose and that we were not aware of this purpose when we acted.

Second, an agent's ability to articulate what he intends in his action, the rule that he adopts for his performance, may be limited. The example offered earlier was that of a painter who could not describe in detail the outcome he intends on the canvas. His attention to line, color texture, and space involves constant critical assessment and refined judgment, but he cannot articulate with precision the rule (or rules) that govern his performance. In our everyday activity we are more like this artist than is usually acknowledged. We make a multitude of critical discriminations between particular possibilities for action, but we cannot always articulate fully the rules employed in those judgments. We may know how to regulate our performance critically without knowing that the principle of this regulation can be given a particular formulation.[8] We may, for instance, be unaware of *specific details* of the rule we are following (e.g., the pattern of a young man's choices of female companionship may reveal that the woman he seeks must, among other things, be able to make him feel important). Or we may be unable to recognize the *overall "shape"* of a rule of action (e.g., taken as a whole the young man's preferences suggest that the woman he seeks must be just like his mother). The agent will be able to offer *some* correct description of his intention (e.g., to invite Mildred to the dance, to drop Mildred and take up with Eunice), but the longer-range intention at work in these actions (e.g., to find a woman just like mother) may remain quite opaque to the agent. This is most often true of long-term intentions that organize a wide range of an agent's activities and so are pervasively at work in his particular actions. An individual may need the help of others, a great deal of reflection, and some further experience before he is able to recognize that a series of actions can be understood by referring them all to an overarching intention, a common rule of action, of which he had been unaware.

This is not, of course, a complete account of all the phenomena with which a psychologist or psychiatrist is concerned in talk of subconscious aims. The purpose of this discussion is merely to see whether it is logically possible to talk of intentions in action of which the agent is unaware. It seems clear that we can and do speak of such intentions. An agent will often not be able to give a complete description of every project in which his particular performance has a place. Except in certain special cases, however, an agent who acts intentionally will be able to give at least a partial description of the project he has undertaken.[9]

4. INTENTION AND THE AGENT'S REGULATION OF ACTION

The concept of intention in action is inextricably bound up with the concept of regulation of behavior in accord with one's intentions. This is the second of the two key points with which we began. I have suggested that an agent's intention in action can best be understood as a rule that he adopts for his performance. This supposes that an agent is able to legislate for his own behavior, prescribing the pattern of his performance. To intend behavior of a particular description is not simply to foresee and desire the occurrence of behavior fitting that description, but is also to commit oneself to undertaking behavior that conforms to that description.

I might be aware that when a doctor strikes my knee with his rubber hammer I will display behavior of the description "extending the lower part of my leg." While this behavior satisfies a description of which I am aware in advance and though it is a behavior that I may want to display (if I want to have normal reflexes), it is hardly intentional. I do not make behavior of that description a program of action to be carried out, and I do not regulate my performance so as to satisfy that description. A malicious patient, however, might plan to so exaggerate his response to the blow on his knee that he kicks the doctor squarely in the chest. It may then happen that when the doctor strikes the patient's knee the patient reacts so suddenly and with such unexpected force (perhaps because he is feeling jumpy in anticipation of trying to carry out his hostile scheme) that he kicks the doctor just as he had planned. Again, this behavior is not intentional, even though he had planned to do just as he did and even though we could say that his intention to kick the doctor caused him (by agitating him) to kick the doctor, for though his behavior conformed to the description under which he had intended to act, he never executed his plan.[10] It is not enough that one intend the performance of behavior of description A at time T and display that behavior at that time.[11] If that behavior is to be an intentional action, it must conform to the agent's intention (i.e., to the rule he has adopted for his performance) because he regulates his behavior so as to conform it to his intention.

A closely related point emerges in considering action ordered to bringing about, through one's bodily performance, some state of affairs or event as the end result of one's performance, such as when I move my body in certain ways in order to throw a basketball through a hoop. I do not, and indeed cannot, make it my intention simply that a state of affairs obtain or an event occur. Rather, if I intend that some event take place, then I intend that an action of mine result in the occurrence of that event. We do speak of intending that an event occur (e.g., that the ball go through the hoop), but this is shorthand for intending that this event be something I bring about (e.g., by shooting the ball through the hoop). A basketball player may *desire* or *wish* that the ball go through the hoop without specifying in any detail by what agency it do so (e.g., by any member of his team), but if he is to *intend* that it go through the hoop, he must intend that *he* put it through the hoop or that he have someone (acting as his "agent") do so for him. He intends the dropping of the ball through the hoop as an outcome of *his action,* whether that action be "taking a shot" or "asking the seven-foot center to 'dunk it.' " The end that an agent seeks is not simply that a desirable event occur, but that this event be brought about through his agency.[12]

Intention will always be intention to determine what one takes to be determinable (e.g., the direction that I move, the flight of a basketball toward the basket). An agent can only predict but not intend what he takes to be determined in such a way that he cannot effectively intervene.[13] He cannot intend, that is, what he believes is "beyond his power" to bring about. This is a logical point (about the concept "intention") that contains a psychological element (about the beliefs of the agent). I am not denying that people set out to do what is in fact beyond their capacity to achieve, but I am denying that it makes sense to speak of an agent intending an event E if he is convinced that E is unattainable. He might desire, want, wish, or hope for E, but if he *intends* E, then he treats E as achievable through his action. One of the ways of falsifying a person's claim to believe that an action is beyond his power would be to cite an attempt on his part to undertake that action. If an agent professes to intend an action and also professes to find that action utterly beyond his power, then he either does not in fact believe that the action is beyond his power or his behavior is intelligible only under another description (e.g., "proving that this action is beyond my power," "testing my capacities," "ensuring a failure," etc.).

Have we defined intentional action in such a way that "intentional action" is equivalent to "voluntary action"? To say so as a flat assertion would be both unilluminating and controversial, for the distinction between "voluntary" and "involuntary" behaviors has so many different uses that, without careful qualification, it has no light to shed on our talk of intentional regulation of action. Basic bodily functions (e.g., circulation of the blood, movement of oxygen and sugars through cell membranes, etc.) and "stray" body movements (e.g., twitches, jerks) are paradigms of one sense of "involuntary" behavior. In quite a different sense, things that happen to us and in which we are passive or ineffectual—things that we neither do intentionally nor do unintentionally—are spoken of as involuntary (e.g., a swimmer is involuntarily carried out to sea by the tide). Again, things that we do on purpose but are forced, or coerced, to do by circumstance, other persons, or institutions are commonly termed involuntary (as when a business is forced into bankruptcy by a declining economy or when an individual is forced to testify before a grand jury). And again, things one does under some psychological "compulsion" are done involuntarily (as in some cases of special pleading for the "mentally incompetent" criminal).

Given all of these significantly different applications of "voluntary" and "involuntary," it adds nothing very definite to talk of intentional regulation of action to say that all intentional action is voluntary. Some of our behavior may be voluntary in one of these senses and yet not be intentional (e.g., unintended but acknowledged consequences of intentional actions, and behavior in which I merely acquiesce).[14] On the other hand, some of our behavior will be intentional action but will not be voluntary in one of the above senses (e.g., the mobster may not go before the grand jury voluntarily, but neither is his behavior unintentional). Finally, some intentional actions will be voluntary in one of these senses and involuntary in another (again, consider the example of the mobster whose appearance before the grand jury is voluntary insofar as it is not a mere reflex or a mere occurrence or an unintentional action, but is involuntary insofar as it is something he is compelled to do "against his will"). To say that all intentional actions are voluntary will only generate confusion unless we specify the relevant sense of "voluntary."

5. INTENTIONAL ACTION AND FREEDOM

We should not leave this question quite so quickly, however. The question about the status of intentional action with regard to voluntary/involuntary distinctions arose in light of our discussion of intentional regulation of behavior. Another way of stating the concern expressed by that matter is to ask whether we have defined intentional action in such a way that it is logically inconsistent to say both that a behavior is an intentional action and that it is "causally determined." Is the concept of intentional action conceptually tied to freedom of action? Just as "voluntary" did not have a single and unproblematic sense, neither do the apparent contraries "determined" and "free." A great deal of philosophical energy has been invested in exploring the various specific senses in which these terms can be opposed and reconciled. We cannot do justice to that discussion in a short space. But we do need to consider briefly the sense or senses in which the account we have given of intentional action requires that intentional action be free and allows that it may be determined.

G. E. M. Anscombe remarks that she "once saw some notes on a lecture of Wittgenstein in which he imagined some leaves blown about by the wind and saying 'Now I'll go this way . . . now I'll go that way' as the wind blew them."[15] Are these statements declarations of intention? Part of the point of this allegorical example, Anscombe suggests, is to point out that questions about "freedom of action" might be separated from a discussion of intention in action.[16] I think it true that some questions about human freedom can be ignored in discussing intentional action, but if we are to have a concept "intention" that does not reduce to wishing or predicting that certain events will occur, then we cannot do without "freedom" in the limited sense required by allowing an agent the capacity to order behavior with an end (outcome_1) in view. This can be seen by attending more carefully to Wittgenstein's leaves.

The statement "Now I will blow this way" might well have issued from the following line of thought: "I know I move whichever way the wind blows. The wind is blowing south. I will move this way (south)." One would not ordinarily say that this final statement is a declaration of intention. It seems more appropriate to say that in this context the statement "I will blow south" is a prediction about movements that will occur in the immediate future, a prediction based upon knowledge of the crucial factors determining such changes. A regular relation has been noted between the direction the wind blows and the direction the leaf moves. The statement "I will move this way (south)" is a simple deduction from this generalization. If an explanation of the prediction is called for, this generalization and deductive inference can be presented as a justifying argument. If one wishes to challenge the correctness of the prediction, one can question the reliability of the generalization or ask whether the condition it correlates with the predicted event in fact now obtains. Once the movement south has occurred, a question about *why* it took place can be adequately answered by citing its cause (i.e., the north wind).

On the other hand, the statement "Now I will move this way

(south)" may have issued from a rather different context of thought, namely, "The direction that I move is something that I can control to some degree. I will move south." Here the final statement is a declaration of intention. If the first of the leaf's claims is correct, then no inference from a wider pattern of events is necessary for the speaker to know that his second statement is correct. Nor is it necessary to display such an inference in order to certify that statement to others. The question "What makes you think you will move south?" either (1) fails to recognize the original statement as a declaration of intention, or (2) questions, in an indirect way, the likelihood of success (e.g., "What makes you think you can get over the wall?"). In the former case the question is correctly answered by a restatement of the intention such as "I have decided to move south." In the latter case, a prediction is being made (or the prediction of success suggested by the declaration of intention is being questioned), and an appropriate response points out features of one's anticipated procedure in acting, aspects of the situation relevant to the success of the undertaking, and so on. When one calls for justification of the statement "I will move south," one will not in this case be calling for a justification of the individual's claim to *know* that he will move south. Rather one will be calling for a justification of his decision to *undertake* such a movement. He will not answer by showing how the statement follows from some empirical generalization, but rather by explaining his interest in this action—by citing his broader intentions in this behavior, by filling in some of the background motivation of this choice, by noting the general policy it enacts, and so on.

Now let us suppose that the leaf that declared its intention to move south was wrong about its capacity to regulate its movements intentionally. All of its movements are in fact determined by the direction the wind blows. Its decision to move south is (we shall say) determined by its "wind direction sensing mechanisms." Its statement of intention to move south is simply a symptom of the fact that the wind is blowing south with sufficient velocity to move it. The rules for action it adopts, therefore, will always correspond to the direction that the wind blows. Given this situation, the leaf can go on indefinitely thinking that it regulates at least some of its movements and prize itself the agent of intentional actions. Its concept of intentional action would be compatible with its experience. It adopts a rule for action, and its performance conforms to that rule. But its concept of intentional action is not compatible with knowledge of what its situation is in fact. It is not itself actually an instance of what it understands by "intentional agent," for its concept of intentional action requires not simply that an agent's performance satisfy a rule but rather that the agent follow a rule, that he regulate his performance in conformity to that rule. The leaf, however, cannot be said to regulate its behavior in accord with its intention, the rule it adopts for action; rather, its intentions register the occurrence and direction of events that it cannot control but that determine its movements (and its "intentions"). There is no sense in which the leaf moves as it does because it has adopted the rule for action "move south." Its intention has no explanatory value, but is itself a phenomenon to be explained in terms of antecedent causal conditions.

On certain physical determinist accounts of human thought and action, the predicament of human beings is in some important respects precisely that of the leaf blown by the wind. A physical determinist might suggest, for example, that an individual's intentions (and all his thoughts, feelings, perceptions, etc.) are merely epiphenomena of causally determined neurological processes. In that case our deliberation, decision, and action are strictly functions of neurological events which proceed according to general laws. Given a complete knowledge of relevant neurological events prior to some time T_1, these general laws would allow us to deduce what neurological events will occur at T_2, since each constellation of neurological events "causally necessitates" the next.[17] As the epiphenomena of such events, our intentions are entirely dependent for their content and development upon the causally necessitated flow of neurological process. Neurological processes, along with the environmental events that trigger those processes, constitute the necessary and sufficient conditions for each moment of consciousness and each movement of the body.[18]

A good deal would need to be said in elaboration of this determinism before its plausibility (or even conceptual possibility) could be assessed.[19] The point to be made here, however, is this: it did not seem possible to say *both* that all the leaf's movements are determined by the direction of the wind *and* that some of the leaf's movements are intentional actions. Neither does it seem possible to say *both* that all human behavior is determined solely by a chain of causally necessitated neurological events *and* that some human behavior is intentional action, for if my intention is simply an epiphenomenon of causally determined neurological processes, then there is no sense in which I act as I do because those actions carry out my intention. My behavior cannot be explained by appeal to my intention as a prescriptive rule, or norm, for my performance. Rather, a complete explanation of my performance can be given strictly in terms of antecedent neurological conditions that causally necessitate each movement in that performance.

This causally necessitated sequence of movements, sounds, and so on will no doubt constitute an overall pattern of behavior that is focused and functional. At the very least, the neurophysiological structures of a viable organism will establish patterns of behavior (in response to environmental stimuli) that are biologically successful. We might well look at segments of an animal's behavior that are biologically successful (e.g., the seasonal migration of a bird species) and say that those behaviors are performed *in order* to meet the biological needs of the organism (e.g., the need to live within a certain temperature range). But on any strict application of the physical determinist's hypothesis, this will amount to explaining the *function* of those behaviors in the overall "economy" of causally necessitated biological processes that constitute the animal's life. Given the physical determinist's suppositions, we can never ascribe a purpose to behavior in any sense other than this (viz., function within a wider causal system). It will never be possible to explain behavior in terms of purposes *qua* rules, or norms, that prescribe correct performances for an agent. We can only explain behavior in terms of purposes *qua* functions of behavior in a system of causally interconnected processes. The behavior of such an organism can *have* a purpose (i.e., a function) but cannot be performed *on* purpose or *for* a purpose. We can never say that an organism regulates its performance so as to *follow* a rule. We can only say that its activities (and interests, decisions, projects, expectations, etc.) are causally regulated so as to *exemplify* a rule (i.e., a rule of regular sequence expressible as an empirical generalization).

On the physical determinist's account, then, human behavior is causally necessitated by factors extrinsic to one's intention just as the behavior of the leaf was. We human beings, like the leaves, may well fancy ourselves the agents of our actions. It is possible, if we are ignorant of the description that the physical determinist would give of our situation, to believe (mistakenly) that we regulate our behavior in accord with our intentions. But talk of intentional action will trade, in the physical determinist's world, upon an appearance of intentional control over our behavior which we do not in fact exercise.

It is worth noting that in a physical determinist's world we need not abandon talk of undertaking action intentionally, any more than talk of the sun rising and setting need be discontinued once the sun is recognized to be at the center of our solar system. When the sun was thought to rotate around the earth, the statement "The sun rises in the east and sets in the west" was taken to be a correct description of processes taking place each day in the universe. But once the earth was displaced from its central and motionless position, talk of the sun rising and setting became a colloquial expression from which no inferences could be drawn about the structure of the universe. If someone now begins to draw such inferences, we correct him by pointing out that it *appears* that the sun rises and sets *to us* who are on the surface of a globe that spins on its axis. So too, once the physical determinist has convinced us of the correctness of his account of our behavior, we will not infer from a description of behavior as intentional action that an agent has made behavior of that description a program of action to be carried through; rather, this expression would be a conventional idiom from which no conclusion could be drawn about the capacity of persons to regulate their performances intentionally. What we experience as "acting in accord with our intentions" is now recognized to be a causally necessitated physiological reaction rooted in environmental stimuli and accompanied by a felt sense of the aim (outcome$_1$) of the behavior—just as the leaf, blown south by the wind, experiences its motion as "setting out in a southerly direction."[20]

If a determinism of this sort is incompatible with the idea of intentional action, it does not follow that intentional actions are free. One might reject physical determinism of this sort, allow that an agent regulates his behavior in accord with his intentions, and yet insist that what an agent intentionally undertakes is determined by his wants and aversions, his inclinations and disinclinations. This would involve arguing that the focusing of an agent's attention upon one project rather than another is causally necessitated by antecedent psychological events. Deliberation and decision would reduce to a process of adjusting competing inclinations and disinclinations according to their various "strengths." General laws could in principle be stated, and these laws, if combined with a correct description of antecedent psychological factors (e.g., desires, aversions, and relevant beliefs), would conceivably allow us to deduce what an agent will intentionally undertake.

A psychological determinism of this general type appears to be compatible with talk of intentional action. An agent does, on this account, critically regulate his performance in accord with the project he intends. In fact, such a determinism might be proposed as a way of explaining the "mechanism" of an agent's intentional regulation of his behavior: one might suggest that the behavior that carries out an agent's intention is caused by his desire to perform behavior of that description.[21] To say, however, that a determinism of this general sort may be compatible with talk of intentional action, is not to say that it can do justice to the full range of our concerns in talk of moral responsibility and freedom. I want to leave these questions open. The primary point here is that a psychological determinism, but not a physical determinism of the type we have discussed, can allow talk of regulation of behavior in accord with one's intention and so be compatible with the concept of intentional action.

A LOOK AHEAD

The discussion to this point has had a deductive structure. We considered the necessary conditions for the use of character trait predicates and found that the behavior appraised by these terms must be intentional action. We then found that if behavior is to count as intentional action it must be regulated in accordance with a rule that expresses the agent's intention for his behavior. The concept of intentional action, therefore, is logically tied to the concept of an agent, an individual who is able to regulate purposefully at least some stretches of his own activity. We now must turn our attention to this concept of an agent and ask whether and how we might develop an account of God as an agent.

Our discussion at this point divides naturally into two stages. First, we need to sift through some of the central issues that dominate efforts to understand human agency. Second, we can then explore the ways in which our understanding of persons as agents might be put to work in thinking about God as an agent.

A useful point of orientation for the first stage of our discussion has been located by the deliberations of this chapter. The concept of an agent, I have argued, is the concept of an individual capable of intentionally regulating at least some of his own behavior. I have not taken up the question, even in general terms, of how we are to explain the agent's capacity to act intentionally. If my arguments here have been sound, the assertion that an agent does intentionally regulate the behavior that constitutes his action is grounded in the logic of the concept "intentional action." Particular explanatory hypotheses about the agent's intentional self-regulation will not have this status, however, unless a convincing case can be made for the unlikely claim that one of these proposals is entailed by the very concept of intentional action. It should be possible, then, to limit the extent of our commitment to any particular theoretical account of the agent's capacity to regulate his behavior intentionally and yet speak of this capacity without begging any of the conceptual questions that are our chief concern.

We must locate ourselves, however, at least with regard to the choice between dualistic and nondualistic accounts of the agent's intentional control of action. One very important type of proposal about how persons operate as agents trades upon a radical distinction between mind and body as separate substances conjoined in a human life. If one accepts this mind-body dualism as an apt account of the human agent, then an array of distinct possibilities are opened up for the second phase of our deliberations. The concept of mind as an active but immaterial entity promises to be useful in thinking about God as an unembodied agent active in or upon the world. Dualist accounts of intentional action, however, have been subjected to a number of acute criticisms. If mind-body dualism is rejected, not only must theological proposals that trade upon it be given up, but a broader question arises about the possibility of speaking of an agent who is not inherently bodily (i.e., who is not a psychophysical unit). This, of course, poses a fundamental challenge to traditional forms of theism.

In the two chapters of Part Two we will take a look at the way a mind-body dualist understands the human agent, discuss some of the most telling criticisms of this account, and consider the broader consequences for theology of rejecting mind-body dualism. Then in

Part Three we will sketch out an account of the human agent as a psychophysical unit and explore the uses of these nondualist person concepts in theology.

PART TWO

Minds, Bodies, and God

CHAPTER 3

Dualism and Divine Mind

1. MIND-BODY DUALISM

> Now I know that I exist, and at the same time I observe absolutely nothing else as belonging to my nature or essence except the mere fact that I am a conscious being; and just from this I can validly infer that my essence consists simply in the fact that I am a conscious being. It is indeed possible (or rather, as I shall say later on, it is certain) that I have a body closely bound up with myself; but at the same time I have, on the one hand, a clear and distinct idea of myself taken simply as a conscious, not an extended, being; so it is certain that I am really distinct from my body, and could exist without it.[1]

In this way Descartes articulates the dualism that has come under sustained attack in contemporary philosophy. Persons are a composition of two substances: mind and body. These substances are inherently distinct, independent, and complete, however intimately bound together they may be in the lives of human beings. Considered in themselves, apart from their actual association in a human life, neither of these substances bears any essential relation to the other; rather, each possesses essential characteristics that are excluded by the other. The essential characteristic of matter, or body, is extension in space. The essential characteristic of mind is "thought," broadly understood to embrace all the contents and operations of consciousness. The distinction between mind and body is radical: it is a distinction between substance that is thinking and unextended on the one hand, and substance that is extended and unthinking on the other.

The body is a mechanical system that operates according to universal laws governing the motions of matter. Accordingly, the body is subject to causal determination by the matter with which it interacts. Beyond this, however, human bodies are subject to determination by the mental substance with which they are associated. Minds have a status as causes parallel to that of material things. The human body may be moved either by the motions of matter or by the initiatives of mind. If the ruling causality in any particular motion is the mind and its energizing acts, then bodily movement is intentional action. But if a bodily movement results strictly from the interaction of material bodies, then it is a mere automatism. The distinction between action and happening is a distinction in orders of causation.

This makes possible a relatively simple account of the agent's intentional regulation of bodily behavior. Intentional action can be analyzed into two components: a mental act and an outward bodily movement. These events are distinct, just as mind and body are distinct, and they bear a relation to one another as cause and effect. I "will" that a bodily movement take place, and it does so, within the limits of the bodily mechanism I command. Bodily movement follows from my mental act of "willing" as an effect from its appropriate cause.

In performing a bodily action, what one does most directly is the mental act of willing, which results in the movement of the body. Bodily movement merely displays outwardly the effect of inner mental initiatives. Accordingly, it is the mental act that is appraised as wise or generous, imperceptive or self-seeking. The bodily movement alone is not susceptible to such appraisal; it becomes appraisable by these predicates only when considered in terms of its cause (i.e., an act of will). Character trait predicates are ascribed to mind—not to body or to mind and body in conjunction—for mind is the agent of wise or generous actions, and is the "I," or self, that is the subject of such characterizations. It is I who act wisely or generously, I who possess and display traits of character. And, Descartes would have us say, "I am really distinct from my body, and could exist without it."

2. CRITICISM OF MIND-BODY DUALISM

The critique of mind-body dualism is well-traveled territory in contemporary philosophy; running through it has become something of a warm-up exercise for philosophers. My purpose here is not to reissue a standard array of old arguments. We need to have an accurate grasp of the crucial objections to dualist theory of action if we are to assess the impact of rejecting dualism upon the theological project of conceiving of God as an agent of intentional actions.

The Interaction of Mind and Body. Some of the principal objections to the dualist's proposals have been with us for some time. No sooner were the *Meditations* read by Descartes's contemporaries than questions arose about the interaction of mind and body. "I beg you to tell me," wrote Princess Elizabeth in 1643, "how the human soul can determine the movement of the animal spirits in the body so as to perform voluntary acts—being as it is merely a conscious (pensante) substance."[2] In one form or another, that question has dogged dualism whenever its key distinction has been proposed. Descartes's own responses to it range from his inevitably unsatisfactory theories about the pineal gland to a frank acknowledgment of the underlying conceptual difficulty. "It seems to me," he wrote back to Princess Elizabeth, "that the human mind is incapable of distinctly conceiving both the distinction between body and soul and their union, at one and the same time."[3] The problem is not simply that we lack an adequate theory to account for the interaction of mind and body; rather, the crucial difficulty is that once mind and body have been radically distinguished as substances defined by incompatible essential characteristics, it is hard to understand how they could interact—and it is even harder to make sense of the suggestion that "the two are so closely joined together that they form, so to speak, a single thing."[4]

The Obscurity of "Volitions." Let us suppose, however, that philosophical reflection points to the necessity of distinguishing between mind and body as inherently independent substances, even though it may then be difficult to explain their relationship in a human life. The interaction of these quite different substances will be a theoretically impenetrable mystery, but it will also be a practical certainty, irrefutably established by our experience. "It is just by means of ordinary life and conversation, by abstaining from meditating and from studying things that exercise the imagination, that one learns to conceive the union of soul and body."[5] Now, one of the points in ordinary life at which we are assured that mind and body interact is in our intentional bodily actions. Here the initiatives of mind cause certain bodily movements to occur. We should be able to give an account of the mental events that cause bodily motion even if we cannot explain *how* they are able to cause these motions, for during our waking hours we are almost always engaged in some intentional bodily action. The mental events that cause these bodily actions should be a prominent feature of our conscious lives.

This does not turn out to be the case, however. It is not at all clear just which features of our conscious operations we should identify as volitions, or acts of will. Do we "will" by imagining and anticipating a bodily movement, by issuing a self-addressed command (e.g., "Arm, be raised!"), by articulating and confirming a desire in the form of a self-addressed declaration (e.g., "I want to raise my arm")? It appears that any or all of these might be present without the appropriate bodily action being undertaken. Initiation of intentional action does not seem to be associated in every case with any one of these mental acts. Neither singly nor together do they constitute sufficient conditions for undertaking action.

The dualist can respond, of course, that there is a particular type of imagining, commanding, or wanting that always issues in the bodily movements that are imagined, commanded, or wanted. But then he must produce an identifying description of this type of mental act, and it seems unlikely that he will find any way of doing so that does not beg the question. It will not do to define the class of mental acts that invariably cause bodily action as "That set of imaginings, commandings, or wantings that in every case cause bodily action." This does nothing to identify this class of mental acts in terms of distinctive features of their content or character as mental acts. Rather, it identifies them in terms of the function that the dualist's hypothesis assigns to them, and so simply restates the hypothesis. The question remains whether there are in fact any mental acts that have this function. The dualist has great difficulty in directing us to such mental acts so that we can, as it were, "see for ourselves." Given Cartesian claims that mind, upon reflection, is better known than body, the obscurity of these mental acts is especially damaging.

Volition and Infinite Regress. Though the dualist is unable to shed much light on the characteristic content of the mental events that cause bodily action, he is likely to insist upon the status of these events as intentional acts performed by mind in order to move the body. Intentional bodily action is treated as a causal sequence having a mental "act of will" as its initial cause and a movement of the body as its final effect. The origination of this causal sequence in an intentional mental act distinguishes the resulting bodily motion from a mere change, or happening, determined by laws governing the motions of matter. If a movement of the body is to count as an intentional action it must be caused by an act of willing that the bodily movement take place.

Must the dualist go on to say that in order to will that the bodily action take place one must first perform an act of willing to will that the action take place? We may well think so, for the dualist appears to be suggesting that for an event to be an intentional action it must be caused by a prior mental act of will—but in that case, an act of will must itself be the effect of a causally prior mental act. This, of course, leaves us with an infinite regress of willings to will that make it impossible ever to undertake any intentional action. The theory of volitions, then, reduces to absurdity.

3. TWO WAYS OF AVOIDING INFINITE REGRESS

We must not conclude too quickly, however, that we have caught the dualist in this *reductio.* Dualism will give way to an infinite regress of volitions only if the dualist affirms both of the following propositions: (1) acts of will are themselves intentional actions, and (2) every intentional action must be caused by an act of will. Taken together, these propositions do generate an infinite regress of willings to will, but it is open to the dualist to deny either or both of them.

Desire as Cause of Action. Strictly speaking, it may not be possible to deny the first proposition as it is stated. Depending upon the definition of "act of will," the phrase "unintentional act of will" might be a contradiction in terms. Be this as it may, it *is* an open option for the dualist to abandon the notion of volitions altogether. His dualism commits him to a causal account of mind-body interaction in intentional action, but it does not commit him to the particular causal account that we have discussed.

The dualist might propose that subintentional mental events of one sort or another cause the bodily movements that are intentional actions. He might claim, for example, that events of desiring, or wanting, to perform some action or achieve some outcome cause bodily actions to be undertaken. Unlike the declaration of desire that we mentioned as a possible content for mental acts of will, these "desirings" or "wantings" are *not* something an agent does intentionally. Whatever particular account one gives of how desires arise, they will have a status *more like* that of feelings and bodily sensations (which occur without being intended) than like that of the deliberate intellectual acts that were postulated as "volitions." But while desires cannot be described as "intentionally undertaken," the bodily behavior in which they issue can be so described. To act intentionally, on this account, is to act in accord with one's desires or wants. A proposal of this sort would clearly face a number of potentially decisive difficulties, some endemic to its underlying dualism (e.g., problems about the interaction of mind and body, problems about the possibility of ever knowing what desires are experienced by others), and some peculiar to the array of concepts it employs (e.g., problems about treating desires as discrete events, problems about identifying the class of causally effective desires). Further, a desire-as-cause theory leads, perhaps inevitably, to a thorough psychological determinism.

I will not explore in detail this dualistic desire-as-cause theory of action. Suffice it to say that the possibility of a desire-as-cause proposal illustrates my point that the dualist is not committed, simply by distinguishing mind and body in the way he does, to a theory of volitions that generates an infinite regress.

Unwilled Acts of Will. If the dualist affirms the first of the two propositions noted above, that acts of will are themselves intentional actions, then he will undoubtedly want to deny the second in order to avoid the absurdity of an infinite regress. There is nothing in his distinction between mind and body or in his affirmation of the first proposition that logically requires him to affirm the second as well. As a result, the dualist who talks of "volitions" is not inevitably drawn into an infinite regress of acts of will. In this respect, Ryle's well-known argument against dualist volition-theory fails, for it begs the question of whether every intentional (or in the terms of Ryle's discussion, "voluntary") action, including mental acts, must issue from prior volitions.[6] The dualist need not commit himself to this proposition. Specifically, he can deny that every act of will has a prior act of will as its cause while insisting that all intentional *bodily* actions are caused by acts of will.

If, however, the dualist denies that *every* intentional action must be caused by an act of will, we might well wonder why we should say that *any* intentional action is caused by an act of will (in the sense that the dualist gives to this phrase). If mental acts need not be caused by prior acts of will, why should we say that bodily actions are brought about this way? For the dualist, of course, the answer is to be found in his dualism. Propelled by his radical distinction between mind and body, the dualist must give a causal account of the interaction of mind and body in intentional action. If he is to avoid the psychological determinism generated by treating the mental causes of action as subintentional episodes of desiring, then he must appeal to intentional mental acts performed in order to move the body (i.e., volitions).

If we abandon the dualist's identification of mind and body with inherently different substances, then we have no need and no occasion to talk of acts of will in the sense of intentional actions of mind distinct from and necessary for the production of intentional bodily movements. Jettisoned along with the concept of volitions is the embarrassment of giving a central place in one's theory of action to events that according to the theory ought to be a pervasive feature of our conscious experience but which in fact cannot be clearly identified at all. And in dropping dualism one sheds as well the exaggerated paradoxicalness that attaches to incarnate mental life once the dualist has made his distinctions.

The dualist might respond that the distinction between mind and body, coupled with the postulation of mental acts of volition, gives us a way of explaining how intentional bodily actions are initiated and guided. The theory of mental acts of will, he could claim, gives us a useful insight into the mechanisms of intentional regulation of bodily performances. Nothing is gained, however, by introducing mental acts of volition. While intentional regulation of bodily action is explained by reference to causally effective volitions, intentional control of those volitions is not itself explained by appeal to prior volitions. Rather, volitions are treated as intentional actions that an agent performs without having to do anything else first in order to bring about those actions. But this is precisely the status that intentional bodily action itself will have if reference to volitions is eliminated. The postulation of volitions only postpones and relocates questions about how we are to understand the agent's intentional regulation of those actions that are not themselves controlled by anterior, causally effective performances. Volition theory does not provide any additional explanatory insight into these actions, though we have seen that it does introduce some novel difficulties.

Mind-body dualism, then, has little to recommend it. Its promise of insight into human action remains unfulfilled, while its fundamental distinction introduces a number of perplexing problems. Mind-body dualism does direct attention to certain key issues in theory of action; for example, our discussion of dualism has located the point at which questions about the agent's intentional regulation of his actions arise most decisively, namely, in considering those intentional actions that an agent can undertake without first performing any more simple action as the means of enacting his intention. But the dualist's theoretical proposals face widely recognized difficulties that have prompted a search for less problematic schemes for understanding human action.

4. DUALISM AND DIVINE MIND

Before we go on to explore a way of understanding persons that does not adopt the dualist's central distinction, we need to consider the impact of rejecting dualism upon the theological project of conceiving of God as an agent of intentional actions. There are two general points that I will develop in the discussion that follows. First, the rejection of mind-body dualism eliminates certain appealing ways of drawing upon our understanding of the human agent to help structure our thought about God as an agent. But, second, in rejecting dualism we are not forced to abandon any claim that is crucial to theism. In particular, none of the arguments that I have offered against dualism so far show that the concept of a nonbodily agent is incoherent or nonsensical.

We can begin to give detail to these claims by noting four complementary ways in which a theologian might put dualist patterns of thought to work in his systematic reflection upon the concept of God. First, if the dualist has given a coherent and compelling account of how we might best think of persons, then the idea of existence as a mental entity will have an indispensable place in the common conceptual equipment that we use or presuppose in our dealings with one another. No concept will be more unavoidable (though many will be easier to grasp) than that of mental substance. Given the familiarity of this notion, there will be no trace of conceptual scandal in talk of a Divine Mind who exists unembodied. We will live in the company of embodied substantial minds, beyond which we can look toward the unembodied Divine Mind.

Second, we will have a pattern on which to understand (or, more accurately, on which to explain our inability to understand) the way in which God acts upon the physical world. If intentional action is analyzed in terms of the operations of a mental entity upon a material entity, neither of which bears any essential relation to the other, then no special problem will arise about the operations of an unembodied God in and upon the world. As Descartes himself suggests in a letter to Henry More,

> Of course I do not think that any mode of action belongs univocally to both God and creatures, but I must confess that the only idea I can find in my mind to represent the way in which God or an angel can move matter is the one which shows me the way in which I am conscious I can move my own body by my own thought.[7]

The impenetrable mystery of Divine Mind acting upon the world it has created will have a precedent in the familiar (though equally impenetrable) mystery of our intentional control over the motions of our bodies. If we tolerate perplexity in the latter as unavoidable, we can hardly reject the former simply for being unfathomable.

Third, there appears to be a precedent for ascribing predicates of perfection drawn from the class of traits of character (e.g., loving-kindness, wisdom, mercifulness, justness) to God as unembodied Divine Mind, for in our own experience the bearer of character traits is mind, or conscious selfhood, alone. All that characterizes us as distinct individuals who are distinctively personal will be associated with our existence and operation as minds. We noted earlier that it is as minds that we act, determining certain movements of the body. This entails that it is as minds that we bear traits of character and a unique personal identity. Hence the idea of an unembodied personal being who is loving or wise or just should not strike us as at all peculiar. We can ascribe these predicates to such a being as long as we can identify certain events as effects that he intentionally produces, just as we ascribe these predicates to persons on the basis of their bodily effects.

This suggests a fourth use of the mind-body dualism, namely, to offer an account of God's hiddenness and self-revelation. We have no immediate access to one another's subjectivity. Since a person is his subjectivity, other persons cannot be known directly. If we are to know what another person feels, desires, or intends, he must disclose himself to us in action or speech. Bodily actions merely make public, indeed "reveal," the personal identity that he bears as a self who is inherently unobservable. Hence talk of God as one whose life lies hidden "beyond" our world and yet who reveals himself in our world will have a direct parallel in the communication that takes place between persons. The degree to which God transcends our grasp and the character of the subjectivity he reveals to us may be unique, but the idea of a being who cannot be known except in his self-disclosure through a medium that is distinct from him (e.g., a body, an action in the world) will be quite familiar to us.[8]

Clearly, these patterns of theological argument will have to be given up if the mind-body dualism upon which they trade is rejected. How serious a loss is this for the project of thinking about God as an agent of intentional actions?

I want to consider in some detail the consequences of abandoning the first of these patterns of argument before turning to the other three more briefly. When mind-body dualism is rejected, what becomes of the notion of Divine Mind? One might argue in the following way. The dualist's hypothesis about persons unravels under the strain of various conceptual difficulties. The source of these difficulties is the claim that mind is an entity, or substance, and a distinct subject of predication. To reject dualism is to refuse to treat mind as that particular part, or sub-entity, within the total person that is the actual subject of predicates like "suffering from a toothache," "shrewd in business," "always generous with friends," and so on. We must now acknowledge that it is the person, not specifically the mind or soul in its activities of controlling the body, who is shrewd in business or generous with friends. Indeed, we now say that it is the person, not a part of the person called mind, who works "mental arithmetic," images a distant place and event, tries to remember the date of Luther's birth, and so on. All of those things that the dualist ascribes to mind (and that fill out the notion of that substance with some concrete content) are now ascribed to the person.

We will want to know more, of course, about the concept of the person employed in this line of reflection. The general shape of the philosophical proposal being made here is easily perceived. The person is *not* a compound of two simpler entities, but is an irreducible unit. If behaviorism is rejected, this unit cannot be a "mere body," an entity that in principle can be the subject only of statements about shape, position, movement, and so on (all statements about thoughts, emotions, intentions, and traits of character being reducible to these terms). Neither is the person a body to which something else has been added—a mind, for instance. We might say that a person is a psychophysical unit. This is a correct and useful bit of terminology, but without further explanation it is not very illuminating. It states in a single term an intention to reject mind-body dualism without slipping into behaviorism. But it does not carry us very far toward understanding what such an entity might be. We are faced, then, with the key claim that a person is neither a mere physical thing nor the product of adding a special psychic entity to a body.

I will suggest in Chapter 5 that it is precisely the concept of intentional action that will allow us to shed light on this concept of the person (i.e., the person can be understood as an agent organism, a body that is capable of intentional action). At this point, however, what interests us is the claim that the person as a unit, not the mind as a part of the person, is the subject of "mental predicates."[9] The concept of mind will take shape in a highly variegated family of properties that we ascribe to a subject that is not itself mind. In light of this, we can argue that there is a category mistake involved in talk of mind as a subject of predication.[10] The concept of mind identifies a set of capacities and characteristics, not a type of substance, or entity. The idea of existence as self-subsistent mind involves a confusion of these categories. The same general type of confusion is involved in saying "You have shown me buildings and grounds, students and professors. Now show me the university to which all of these belong."[11] The notion of existence as mental substance involves this kind of logical mistake, whether the mind is joined to a human body or is posited as the unembodied Maker of heaven and earth.

There are two steps to this argument. First there is the logical point that in talking of mind we are talking of the fitness of a subject to receive predicates of a roughly identifiable family, but are *not* necessarily affirming the existence of a special type of entity. Second, there is the charge that a category mistake is inevitably involved in talk of existence as self-subsistent mind. Taken together, these two points lead to some important conclusions. If both points are granted, then it appears that the subject of mental predicates can only be a person, or psychophysical unit, for when talk of mind as an independent substance is given up, the only available model for a nonbodily subject of mental predicates collapses. This has obvious and important consequences for theological reflection. If this argument is correct, it appears that any reference to a nonbodily subject of mental predicates involves a fundamental conceptual mistake.

This particular argument, however, is easily disarmed. The logical point about the concept of mind is correct. But it is possible to escape the charge that the dualist (or the theist who wishes to speak of a nonbodily subject of mental predicates) inevitably makes a category mistake. We need first to say a little more about the logical point. The concept of mind, I have said, does not name an entity but rather comprises a complex family of things that we say about persons. In the first two chapters we discussed a crucial branch of this family (i.e., traits of character) which included those predicates employed in the evaluation of behavior as intelligent conduct. It is correct to say, I think, that if we are to count an individual as "possessed of mind" (or "minded"), it must be logically possible to ascribe character trait predicates to that individual, since a "minded" individual who is not capable of performances of a type that can be appraised by character trait predicates (i.e., intentional actions), will be nothing more than a purely passive subject of experiences. It can be convincingly argued that the idea of such a subject cannot be formed coherently.[12] In any case, such a subject would not be "minded" in any very significant sense.

The ascribability of traits of character, then, will be a necessary and sufficient condition for asserting that an individual is "minded," at least in the sense in which I will speak of mind. We have seen, however, that traits of character logically require that any subject to which they are ascribed be an agent of intentional actions. Traits of character, I have argued, cannot be ascribed to a "mere body," a physical entity. It is important to note that the logical requirement here, as displayed in the argument of the first two chapters, is that the subject of character trait predicates be an agent, but *not* necessarily that the agent be a body. I argued that traits of character can only be ascribed when some of an individual's performances can be taken under a description of that individual's intentions in his performance. There is nothing in this argument alone that would allow us to conclude that the individual who acts intentionally must in every case be a bodily agent. A further argument, from the necessary conditions for talk of intentional action and agency, would have to be made if this stronger conclusion is to be reached. This argument *does* allow us to conclude, however, that the unitary psychophysical subject to which we ascribe mental predicates must be an agent of intentional actions.

The logical point made by the antidualist argument presented above can now be more exactly expressed by saying that the concept of mind takes shape in a diverse family of predicates that are ascribed to agents on the basis of their intentional actions. The concepts "mind" and "agent" are logically bound together. There can be no "mindless agent," other than in the colloquial sense. And if we do not count the hypothetical purely passive (and therefore unthinking) subject of experiences as "minded," then there can be no "actionless mind." It is important to recognize that in the logical pair "mind" and "agent," "agent" is the subject term and "mind" is a shorthand for a family of capacities and characteristics displayed by agents. Here there emerges the possibility of the "category mistake" referred to in the preceding argument. A category mistake will be involved if one treats "mind" as belonging to the logical category of subjects of predication rather than to the category of families of characteristics. Mind cannot be an entity if that means denying the logical order or shuffling the logical categories of the concepts "mind" and "agent." Proposals involving appeal to minds as distinct entities, whether embodied human minds or unembodied Divine Mind, can be disqualified on conceptual grounds alone if they involve this category mistake.

Neither the dualist nor the theologian, however, needs to contravene this logical structure. Both can modify the terms of their proposals and speak not of mind as a subject of predication, but as an agent to which various mental predicates can be ascribed. The dualist might translate "mind" or "mental substance" into "mental agent," that is, an agent whose immediate actions are always and only processes of thought, memory, decision, volition, and so forth. All bodily actions, for this agent, will be mediated actions; that is to say, they will have an instrumental substructure. Intentional bodily action will always be the outcome intended by an intentionally prior action of the mental agent. The dualist's position, then, could be restated as proposing that a bodily agent is a combination of a mental agent and a bodily mechanism.

This restated dualism will, of course, still face all of the difficulties associated with the way it sorts out and sets apart the mental and the physical in human life. The point here, however, is that as long as the dualist speaks of mind *qua* mental agent he does not make a category mistake, whatever other mistakes he may make. The crucial objection to dualism is that its analysis of persons into two inherently independent entities generates certain irresolvable perplexities. A dualist may offer this analysis because he thinks that mind *qua* the family of mental predicates requires mind *qua* a mental agent as its subject. This is a mistake, but it is not a category mistake: it is not a matter of treating a category of predication as a type of entity. Rather, the mistake is that of assuming that because we can identify a family of characteristics (viz., mental predicates) and distinguish them from another family of characteristics (viz., descriptions of material bodies), there must be two distinct entities to which these characteristics are ascribed. Against this I have suggested that both these families of characteristics can be ascribed to a single subject, namely, the person, or psychophysical unit.

All this suggests that the concept of mind, *qua* a "mental agent," is still available for theological use. A dualistic analysis of the bodily agent may be fraught with difficulties, but the concept of a mental agent—or, more generally, of an agent who is not a psychophysical unit—escapes the charge of making a category mistake. The theologian might recast his talk of "Divine Mind" in terms of a "Divine Agent" without loss, and have a richer and more versatile way of thinking about God as a result.

There is still room, of course, for philosophical suspicion about the idea of an agent who is not a body. The rejection of dualism leads us to wonder whether the concept "agent" is so closely tied to the concept of a psychophysical unit that an agent logically must be a bodily agent. We no longer have easy access to the idea of a mental agent as a component part of the concept of a person, and so are prompted to ask about the intelligibility of this idea. One could argue against dualism that the concept of a mental agent is inconsistent, that one of the necessary conditions for being an agent is being a body (and therefore a psychophysical unit). But none of the arguments we have considered so far take this form or have this force. Our arguments against dualism have shown only that the analysis of the bodily agent into mind and body as distinct constituent substances generates certain conceptual difficulties. I have contended that these difficulties can be avoided, without generating new difficulties beyond those that would have to be faced in any case, by rejecting the dualist's analysis and treating the bodily agent as a psychophysical unit. These considerations may lead us to say that *if* an agent is a *bodily* agent, then that agent must be a psychophysical unit. But an additional argument would have to be offered if we are to reach the more sweeping conclusion that *every* agent must be a psychophysical unit.

In this connection we need to look briefly at a problem that arises when the second of our initial four arguments is given up. When we abandon the dualist's account of intentional action as a causal control of bodily events by mental substance, we can no longer claim a direct analogy between the intrapersonal relation of mind to body and the cosmological relation of God to creatures in divine action. The human agent's control of his bodily performance cannot be cited as a familiar (if little understood) instance of the operation of spiritual substance upon physical substance. Not only is this direct precedent lost, but a problem is raised for the theist, for if mind-body dualism is called into question because it creates problems in understanding how persons act, then talk of God as an agent may be challenged on the same grounds. Can we make sense of the notion of an immaterial divine agent acting in and upon our world? Must an agent be a body in order to act upon bodies? This is a problem that appears straightforward, but immediately fragments upon reflection.

The actions of God to which theistic traditions refer are of various kinds, and raise rather different problems. There is, of course, talk of God's creative activity that establishes creatures in a relation of absolute ontological dependence sustained at every moment of the creature's existence. The problems for thought posed by this relation are enough to make worries about God's actions *in* history pale into insignificance. And then there are those "mighty acts of God in history," God's providential and self-revealing actions within his creation, themselves constituting a diverse class of actions, from Old and New Testament miracles in nature, to the hardening of hearts and the inspiring of prophets, to the central miracles of Christian faith in the incarnation and resurrection of Jesus Christ.

Not all of these claims about divine action are of equal significance for theologians, and not all these types of divine action pose the same problems. As a result, a theologian has a variety of strategies of response open to him.[13] In virtually every case, however, it is appropriate to argue that the theist should not be held responsible to explain the *means* by which God's intentional activity engages his creatures. The obscurity of the "mechanism" of God's activity is just one aspect of the inescapable limits upon our understanding of the activity that constitutes God's life as the divine agent (a claim that I will develop more systematically in Chapters 6 and 7). The point to be made here is that nothing is required of talk of an active relatedness of God to creatures but that such a relation be conceptually possible, that is, neither self-contradictory nor otherwise logically self-disqualifying. Given God's uniqueness as an agent, the means by which his intentional activity engages his creatures must remain a mystery to us, though the effects of his activity and his intentions in bringing about those effects are at least partially captured, for a particular religious tradition, by those descriptions of his actions that are approved and preserved by that tradition. In this case, the theologian can speak with confidence of a mystery that is not reducible to a confusion and deal with imponderables that are not merely a function of conceptual incoherencies.[14]

The third theological use of mind-body dualism (viz., to provide a precedent for talk of an essentially nonbodily personal being) requires only a brief comment in light of what has been said about the first. With the rejection of dualism we will no longer take the subject of character traits and the bearer of a personal identity to be a mental substance that is essentially distinct from the body. We need to be clear, however, about what is lost in giving up this way of thinking. Two of the points that arose in discussing the concept of mind are relevant here. First, the only requirement for the ascription of traits of character that we have identified thus far is that their subject be an agent of intentional actions. It has *not* been shown that the subject of traits of character must be a bodily agent. The logical pattern of ascribing traits of character to an agent on the basis of his intentional actions will hold for *any* agent, whether that agent is or is not a bodily agent. Second, up to this point the arguments presented against mind-body dualism have shown only that the concept of a bodily agent should not be analyzed dualistically. If an agent is a bodily agent, then he will bear his distinctive personal identity as a psychophysical unit, and not as a mind (or mental agent) causally yoked to a body. It remains to be seen whether talk of an agent who is not a psychophysical unit can be ruled out on conceptual grounds.

Finally, a special word is in order about the fourth pattern of argument that I have sketched out. This argument is obviously similar to one developed by Gordon Kaufman in *God the Problem*. Kaufman sets out to offer an account of "transcendence" that avoids an arbitrary opposition between our world and the "beyond." His strategy is to locate some point within our experience at which the concept of transcendence already has a meaning, so that this experienced transcendence can serve as a model for our relation to that which transcends us ultimately. Kaufman finds his preferred model of transcendence in interpersonal relationships. He argues that there are important respects in which a human self is beyond the reach of others' knowledge unless he chooses to make himself known:

> . . . selves always transcend in their subjectivity and freedom what is directly accessible to one in his experience (that is, their bodies). . . . What one directly experiences of the other are, strictly speaking, the external physical sights and sounds he makes, not the deciding, acting, purposing center of the self.
>
> A self in its active center is never directly open to view, but is known only as he reveals himself in communication and communion.[15]

Other persons are not immediately available as objects of knowledge at my disposal. They transcend my cognitive grasp, and can be known only when they open themselves to me. Here, then, is a crucial point in our familiar experience at which talk of transcendence and self-revelation can be readily understood.

Kaufman's critics have argued that this interpersonal transcendence trades upon a "residually Cartesian" understanding of persons.[16] Kaufman's language does seem to trade upon the inner/outer bifurcation that Ryle so thoroughly dismantles. And even a dualist might balk at Kaufman's tendency to say that a person's interiority cannot be known unless that person allows it to be known. In response to his critics, Kaufman has argued that his principal proposals can be disentangled from mind-body dualism. He may underestimate both the extent of the modification that this would require in his interpersonal model and the impact that these changes would have on his other proposals,[17] but he is right in claiming that a nondualistic interpersonal mode of transcendence can be developed. Mind-body dualism merely provides a simple conceptual picture that lends itself to expressing our sense of the immediate "privacy" of subjectivity and the evident fact of subjective distinctness (my experience, thought, and intention are mine alone). We must be careful not to ignore these aspects of our experience when we reject a philosophical view that has made a special claim to them.

If we were to develop an interpersonal model for God's transcendence, however, we would have to give up the claim that intentional self-disclosure, the voluntary making public of what is essentially private, lies at the foundation of all communication between persons. Much of our self-disclosure is *not* deliberately chosen. Being known by others comes along with being a person in a community of persons. We may, in fact, sometimes wish we could be more concealed; we may crave the anonymity of being less well understood. We do not seem to have any great advantage over others in understanding our own character, value structure, and so forth.

Nonetheless, it is also true that we are capable of masking our intentions, hiding our feelings, constructing an identity before others that we do not really claim. It has been remarked often enough since Freud that social existence requires that certain aspects of ourselves not be made public (though this usually requires that we hide them from ourselves as well). In any case, practical experience reminds us that persons have more extensive purposes in their actions than those of which we are aware. Their interests are sometimes complex, idiosyncratic, or obscure. Even when we most want to understand (or be understood by) another person, we often fail to grasp and fully appreciate one another's experience, utterances, and actions. Communication between persons breaks down and we find ourselves tangled in language that confuses and conceals. As a result, we do know what it is for important features of another person's experience to be out of reach. And we do know what it means for one person to open himself to another in an effort to make himself known. We can, therefore, point to a certain "transcendence" that attaches to being a distinct individual, an independent center of experience and action. And we can make sense of the suggestion that a particular action or utterance is peculiarly important in revealing the distinctive character of another person.

Reflection on these features of our experience of persons may well shed light on the transcendence of God as an agent (a) whose life for himself is not exhausted by his life for others and (b) whose actions toward us make him known to us. Real care is required, however, in detailing one's claims about this interpersonal transcendence. Questions about privacy and intersubjectivity are notoriously difficult. In taking up these issues the theologian must pick his way through a region of philosophical discourse that has been hotly contested and so is strewn with loaded language, with words and phrases that have come to signal whole positions. At least some of Kaufman's difficulties come from picking up such language and having it go off in his hands.

If these exploratory reflections are sound, there is every reason to think that a nondualist account of personal interactions will be illuminating for our reflection upon God's transcendence. But I will not center my efforts here on that particular project. My immediate interest is in the consequences of rejecting mind-body dualism for talk of God as a nonbodily agent. The rejection of dualism clearly eliminates certain simple and appealing patterns of theological argument, but the shift to a nondualist understanding of persons does not appear to eliminate any form of reflection crucial to theism. We must give up the notion of mental substance as a fundamental theological category, but we must do so only because the concept of an agent is logically more fundamental. It *would* be troubling to any traditional theism, however, if it could be shown that one of the necessary conditions for being an agent is being a body. Our task in the next chapter is to consider just such an argument.

CHAPTER 4

Embodiment and Identification

1. PERSONS AND LOGICAL PRIMITIVENESS

The critique of mind-body dualism has not yet required that we give up the possibility of conceiving of God as a personal agent who is not a person (that is, not a psychophysical unit). However, in an essay titled "Persons," Peter Strawson has offered some compelling objections to dualism that appear to bear just this more far-reaching consequence.[1] Strawson's essay weaves together several strands of argument against mind-body dualism. One of these may be read as an attempt to disqualify the dualist's understanding of persons by showing that the predicates that define an individual as a purposive agent can be ascribed only to a psychophysical unit. Such a claim, if made good, rules out not only the dualist's notion of substantial mind or mental agency, but also every concept of an agent who is not a psychophysical unit. We need to see what place this claim has in Strawson's arguments and whether a good case is made for it.

The principal concern of Strawson's essay is to display the logical primitiveness of the concept of a person. Both of the key terms here, namely, "persons" and "logical primitiveness," require some initial explanation. By the concept of a person, Strawson means "the concept of a type of entity such that both predicates ascribing states of consciousness and predicates ascribing corporeal characteristics, a physical situation etc. are equally applicable to a single individual of that single type."[2] Strawson never defines with care just what he means to include among "states of consciousness." Later in the essay he defines the person as a single subject of both

"M-predicates" and "P-predicates"—the class of M-predicates consisting "of those which are also properly applied to material bodies to which we would not dream of applying predicates ascribing states of consciousness. . . . They include things like 'weighs 10 stone,' 'is in the drawing-room' and so on," and the class of P-predicates consisting "of all the other predicates we apply to persons." This means that a good deal more than merely states of consciousness (however the class of states of consciousness is delimited) will be counted among P-predicates. Intentional actions and traits of character, for example, will be members of this class. Strawson tells us that "P-predicates, of course, will be very various. They will include things like 'is smiling,' 'is going for a walk,' as well as things like 'is in pain,' 'is thinking hard,' 'believes in God' and so on."[3]

The broader category of P-predicates is not introduced until the basic structure of Strawson's argument has been presented. The argument itself is developed in terms of the necessary conditions for ascribing states of consciousness to any subject. The notion of a class of P-predicates is then introduced as a convenient way of developing one of the conclusions of the argument. Strawson indicates, however, that all P-predicates "imply the possession of consciousness on the part to which they are ascribed."[4] From this it follows that necessary conditions for the ascription of states of consciousness will also be necessary conditions for the ascription of any P-predicate.

Strawson has two rather different ways of explaining what he means by asserting that this concept of a person is "logically primitive." First, he identifies the assertion of logical primitiveness with the claim that "states of consciousness could not be ascribed at all, *unless* they were ascribed to persons, in the sense I have claimed for this word."[5] Although it is not entirely clear how this phrase is to be read, it seems least strained to take it as asserting that states of consciousness can be ascribed *only* to persons. If all P-predicates imply the ascribability of states of consciousness, then it follows that the entire class of P-predicates can be ascribed only to persons (i.e., to psychophysical units). This would have obvious and important implications for our concern with the logical possibility of talk of a nonbodily agent, for it would show that the only possible type of subject to which intentional actions and traits of character (both of which are included in Strawson's class of P-predicates) could be ascribed is a psychophysical unit, a bodily agent. Talk of a personal agent who is not a person (i.e., not a psychophysical unit) would be ruled out on general conceptual grounds.

Second, Strawson identifies the assertion of logical primitiveness with the claim that the concept of a person cannot be analyzed in certain ways—specifically, that it cannot be gotten rid of behavioristically or reduced to simpler constituent elements dualistically. This represents a considerably weaker claim than does the first sense of "logically primitive." It is not being claimed here that persons are the only possible subjects of states of consciousness, but rather that persons are the only possible *embodied* subjects of states of consciousness. If states of consciousness are to be ascribed to a bodily subject, they must be ascribed to the same subject that receives M-predicates. We have already seen that an argument of this limited scope poses no direct challenge to the possibility of talk of an agent who is not a psychophysical unit.

In what follows, I will contend for two basic points. First, Strawson offers no argument that will show that the concept of a person is logically primitive in the strong sense; his arguments could at most establish the weaker claim of logical primitiveness, which nonetheless would be strong enough to achieve the central purpose of his discussion (viz., the elimination of mind-body dualism). Second, Strawson's argument articulates an important logical requirement with which we must come to terms if we are to speak of God as an unembodied agent: it must be possible to identify unambiguously the referent of our talk about God.

2. STRAWSON'S CASE AGAINST DUALISM

We need to take a close look at Strawson's discussion to see if he provides us with any compelling reason to say that the concept "person" is logically primitive in the stronger of the two senses he introduces. Does Strawson's argument against mind-body dualism generate the conclusion that every subject of P-predicates must also be a subject of M-predicates?

Strawson's case against mind-body dualism turns upon three key propositions: first, "one can ascribe states of consciousness to oneself only if one can ascribe them to others"; second, "one can ascribe them to others only if one can identify other subjects of experience"; and third, "one cannot identify others if one can identify them *only* as subjects of experience, possessors of states of consciousness."[6]

Each of these propositions requires some attention. The first is a specific application (to ascriptions of states of consciousness) of a logical rule that, according to Strawson, governs all predication. If I am to ascribe any predicate to myself, it must be logically possible to ascribe that predicate to others. If a predicate is to have a first-person use, it must have a third-person use as well. We will call this the *predication rule*.[7] Strawson argues that the predication rule follows from the very idea of a predicate: "The main point here is a purely logical one: the idea of a predicate is correlative with that of a range of distinguishable individuals of which the predicate can be significantly, though not necessarily truly, affirmed."[8] This is not to say, Strawson notes, that a predicate must in fact be ascribable to more than one individual. It may happen that there is only one individual who is of the appropriate type to receive a particular predicate, or it may happen that there is only one individual of whom it is true to say that the predicate applies. Strawson contends, however, that the logic of predication requires that it be logically possible to ascribe a predicate to more than one individual.[9]

Strawson's second proposition articulates one of the necessary conditions for the ascription of states of consciousness to others: one must be able to identify other subjects of predication. The first half of Strawson's discussion in *Individuals*, including the chapter titled "Persons," is an exploration of the conceptual scheme in terms of which we identify particular things and persons (i.e., particulars). In general, to identify a particular is to make a reference that picks it out as a unique subject of speech. One has not identified a particular if in the same (i.e., numerically identical) circumstances one's reference could be satisfied simultaneously by several particulars. An identifying reference is an individuating reference; it must pick out just one particular as the subject of speech.

The third proposition requires little comment. If I must identify another individual strictly as a subject of experiences, then given the actual inaccessibility of his states of consciousness I will not be able to identify him at all.

In a moment I will raise a question about whether this third proposition fairly represents the dualist's predicament, but first we should note what follows if all three of these points are granted. If the subject to whom states of consciousness are ascribed is *exclusively* a subject of states of consciousness, then third-person ascription becomes impossible (by the second and third premises). But if third-person ascription is impossible, then so is first-person ascription (by the first premise). Therefore, if we think of the subject to whom states of consciousness are ascribed as a subject of states of consciousness alone, then states of consciousness cannot be ascribed *at all*, either in the first or the third person. The conclusion warranted by the argument, in fact, is even stronger than this. Since a subject of states of consciousness alone does not allow for third-person identification, such an individual is not a possible subject of any predication whatsoever.

Clearly this argument hinges on the observation that a subject of states of consciousness alone cannot be identified as a subject of reference. The mind-body dualist will immediately object, however, that this observation has no force against him, for the dualist does not (or need not) say that we identify others *only* as possessors of states of consciousness; rather, we identify others as subjects whose states of consciousness are correlated in certain recognizable ways with the behavior of a body. Mental substance, after all, is conjoined to a body in a human life and interacts with that body in mutual causal interdependence. Given this interaction, however difficult it may be to explain, the dualist will claim that we can perceive the states of an unobservable subjectivity in observable bodily behavior. The dualist might thus grant all three of Strawson's propositions together with the conclusions they generate, since no damage is done to his position unless the indirect identification of other minds through the pattern of their interaction with a body can be shown to be unsuccessful or impossible.

The crux of Strawson's argument, then, lies in his attempt to show that the dualist's indirect identification of other minds involves an egregious logical mistake. The dualist, Strawson contends, cannot identify other subjects of experience without violating the predication rule articulated in the first of the propositions introduced above. According to the dualist, another mind is identified as bearing an interactive relation to a particular human body that is similar to the relation I bear to my body. The crucial identifying relation, therefore, can be secured only by observing the relation of states of consciousness to overt bodily behavior in my own case. This makes the experience in ascribing states of consciousness to myself a necessary condition for ascribing states of consciousness to others. The predication rule, however, states that I can ascribe a predicate to myself only if it is logically possible to ascribe it to others.[10]

Strawson concludes that the analogical identification of other minds generates a vicious circle: I can ascribe states of consciousness to others only if I can ascribe them to myself, but I can ascribe them to myself only if I can ascribe them to others. The necessary conditions for third-person ascription of states of consciousness cannot be met without first-person use (according to the analogical argument), but the necessary condition for first-person use is that I be able to ascribe states of consciousness to others (according to the predication rule). The result is that the necessary conditions for the ascription of states of consciousness can never be met. If we embrace mind-body dualism, then states of consciousness cannot be ascribed at all. And if states of consciousness cannot be ascribed, then neither can any P-predicate whatsoever. The Cartesian ego is not a possible subject of speech.

There are a number of questions that can be raised about this argument, and there is some reason to think that the dualist may be able to slip out of the logical circle in which Strawson has tried to enclose him.[11] But the dualist's self-defense and the various critical responses that might be offered to it are only of secondary interest to us here. For my purposes it is of greater importance to note what would follow from Strawson's argument if it were fully successful. Does this argument warrant the conclusion that persons (in Strawson's sense) are the only possible subjects of P-predicates? The answer clearly is no. Strawson's discussion fastens upon a difficulty that the dualist must face in identifying mental substances. The Cartesian ego can be identified only by appealing to an individuating relation that must be defined in the first person, and this, Strawson tells us, violates the predication rule. If valid, this argument disqualifies the specific individuating relation "the subject of those experiences which stand in the same unique causal relation to body N as my experiences stand to body M," when this relation is the only means of identifying other subjects of experience.[12] More generally, Strawson's argument would show that we cannot ascribe a predicate at all if every possible subject of that predicate can be identified only by appeal to an individuating relation defined in the first person. It is only in this case, if at all, that first-person use would become the necessary condition for any third-person ascription whatsoever. But this is clearly an unusual and restricted case. As long as it is possible to ascribe P-predicates to others without making first-person use the necessary condition of doing so, then there is no reason why at least some of these subjects of predication might not be of a type other than Strawson's "single subject of both M-predicates and P-predicates." In any case, the theistic use of P-predicates will not be dependent upon the particular identifying relation that Strawson's argument eliminates. There may well be significant problems for the theist in identifying God as a referent of P-predicates, but these will be rather different problems than those that Strawson poses for the mind-body dualist.

3. THE IDENTIFIABILITY OF GOD

Strawson's argument does not show that the concept of a person is logically primitive in the stronger of the two senses he introduces; that is, even if his case against the dualist is fully successful, it will not rule out the possibility of reference to a subject of P-predicates who is not a person (i.e., not a psychophysical unit). But his argument does leave us with a logical requirement that any such individual must meet: that individual must be a uniquely identifiable referent of human speech. It must be possible, that is, to give an unambiguous answer to someone who asks, "Who or what are you talking about?" We will not have explained our reference adequately until we have indicated which individual among all the actual and possible contents of our universe we have in mind. If we cannot do this, then we quite literally do not know what we are talking about. The demand for identifiability, then, is a minimum prerequisite for any subject of predication. Can the theist identify the referent of his talk about God when God is understood as an unembodied agent, that is, as a subject of P-predicates who is not also a subject of M-predicates?

In order to answer this question it will be helpful to have before us Strawson's account of the basic scheme of identification at work in references to the contents of our shared world. At the foundation of all our references, Strawson argues, lies the demonstrative identification of particulars in a network of space-time relations. Demonstrative identification picks out linguistically distinguishable items in sense experience (e.g., this tree, that loud noise, etc.). This direct location of particulars within a field of immediate experience provides the foundation for references to more remote objects. If a particular is not present in our immediate field of experience, it may be identified by noting a unique, or individuating, relation it bears to demonstratively identifiable particulars. A relation will be "individuating" only if there is just one particular (of a given description) that bears this relation to our immediate field of experience. Strawson argues that spatio-temporal relations provide an indispensable network of such individuating relations, a network that allows us to broaden the scope of our references beyond particulars present here and now to include objects in remote times and places. The basic scheme of identification with which we operate, then, is constituted by the sensible discrimination of particulars in our immediate environment and by the spatio-temporal relations they bear to other particulars.[13]

If God is understood as an agent who is not a psychophysical unit, then clearly God cannot appear as a subject of reference within this scheme of identifying relations. But if Strawson were to limit the range of possible reference to sensible particulars in space and time, he would be left with an impossibly narrow positivism in which, for example, no reference could be made to states of consciousness (except as a way of organizing information about bodies). While the scheme of demonstrative identification in a spatio-temporal network is foundational, there are other ways in which individuals can be singled out as subjects of predication. Strawson mentions a number of supplementary modes of identification, of which three are relevant to theological concern with identifying reference to God.

First, we might note the possibility of what Strawson terms "story relative identification."[14] It is always possible to identify a particular strictly within the network of terms that a speaker introduces into conversation without making any attempt to give this particular a determinate relation to the field of experience that the speaker and hearer share. A speaker can introduce an array of particulars and construct a narrative framework or systematic conceptual structure in which unambiguous references can be made, but this does not place (locate) any of these particulars in the field of reference radiating out from the shared experiential setting of the speaker and hearer. We simply operate within the imaginative framework that the speaker provides and refer to particulars that appear in this constructed world. We "conspire" with the speaker or author in establishing a field of reference that is not integrated into the universe of particulars that comprises our shared world. "The identification is within a certain story told by a certain speaker. It is identification within his story; but not identification within history."[15]

Story-relative identification in this pure form is clearly of no help to the theologian who does not want to reduce his talk of God simply to an imaginative structure disconnected from the world of particulars in time and space. Theologians typically want to affirm the reality of God, and that requires that God be identifiable not merely as a term in a freely constructed story, but as a possible subject of predication connected with the field of reference to which we ourselves belong. God, however, will not be a demonstratively identifiable entity in space and time. Again, we are confronted with the question of whether our range of references can include God. An exclusively story-relative identification will not help us here. On the other hand, I will suggest below that a modified form of story-relative identification (viz., one which includes reference to particulars within our shared field of experience) does have a significant role to play in talk of God.[16]

A second supplementary mode of identification that crops up in Strawson's discussion is "logically individuating description."[17] A logically individuating description is formulated in such a way that (in principle) it could not be true of more than one individual. For example, I might refer to "the first President of the United States," "the best Austrian violinist," "the only man to survive the battle." Each of these examples relies in various ways on a supporting context to make its reference (e.g., the Presidency must be an office that is filled by only one individual at a time). But given the contexts within which these descriptions make sense, each description admits of satisfaction by only one individual.

Strawson mentions this mode of identification only in passing, and comments on its inherent limitations. Such descriptions do individuate—they do pick out just one individual—but they do not tell us very much about how this individual fits into the field of reference in which we presently have a place. I may not know who was first elected President, what role he played in founding the nation, or that his false teeth now reside in the Smithsonian Institution, but notwithstanding this nearly total ignorance, I can still make an individuating reference to him. One might say that a logically individuating description provides a form that can be filled by just one individual, but does not give us any guidance in indicating which individual fills that form.

In spite of this descriptive incompleteness, this means of identification is theologically important. Some traditional identifications of God have been of this type, and theologians have often been quite candid about their abstractness. The "name" of God that Anselm offers as the first premise of his famous argument functions as a logically individuating description. God is identified as that than which nothing greater can be conceived—that is, as the limiting case of perfection. As with each of the examples of individuating descriptions given above, this description only individuates if certain accompanying conditions are met. It must be allowed that perfection admits of degrees on a continuous scale that has an absolute maximum. And it must be argued that a perfect being will be without equal, that in principle there can be only one instance of maximal perfection. We might say that Anselm's description individuates only in the context of a theological-philosophical story that meets these conditions. Of course, Anselm's name for God does not exhaust the possibilities for individuating description of God. In Chapter 7 I will propose an individuating description that identifies God as a logically singular instance of intentional agency.

If we are to move beyond the inherent abstractness of logically individuating descriptions and give our talk of God some concrete content, then we must connect it more closely to the rest of our experience and references. In light of this, the third supplementary mode of identification is particularly important. This third form of identification is really a class of possibilities. I have noted that the range of our references is extended by citing unique relations that remote particulars bear to demonstratively identifiable particulars in immediate experience; Strawson argues that spatio-temporal relations provide the fundamental network of such relations, but the individuating relation we cite need not in every case be a spatio-temporal relation. For example, Strawson gives a crucial role to a relation of "non-transferable ownership by a single person" in identifying "private particulars" (e.g., states of consciousness).[18] Here a special individuating relation uniquely ties a nonspatial particular to another particular which is itself demonstratively identifiable. The network of sensibly discriminable particulars in space and time remains basic, but these particulars do not exhaust the range of possible references we can make. This suggests that God might be identified by indicating a unique relation that he has to our shared world of objects and events located in space and time. If we think of God as an agent, might we identify God from those events in our experience that are taken to be his acts?[19] The identifying relation in this case is not location in space and time, but rather the relation of an agent and his act.[20]

There are, of course, a number of questions that immediately arise concerning this proposal. The very phrase "act of God" needs clarification. It is not clear what sort of event one has in mind in speaking of such an act. As I noted in the preceding chapter, Western devotional and theological traditions speak of a considerable variety of events as God's acts. It is part of the task of a doctrinal theologian to decide how he will interpret this language about acts of God and to develop a unified view of God's activity in relation to his creation. A broad range of possibilities arises here and poses a variety of different problems for efforts to identify God as an agent. At least two general problems, however, can be outlined briefly.

First, there are problems about identifying the activity that is to be attributed to God as his action. Any uncertainty involved in identifying God's actions will, of course, only compound the difficulties associated with identifying God as the agent of those actions. On most theological accounts God's activity turns out to be more elusive than it may at first appear. Note, for example, one of the central Old Testament events in which God is said to declare himself to man in a special way: the escape of the Hebrew people from slavery in Egypt. Devotional tradition might say, "God rescued the Hebrew people from slavery." How closely parallel is this to saying, for example, "Moses rescued the Hebrew people from slavery"? In the latter case we can indicate more specifically what Moses did in rescuing the Hebrew people: he bargained with and threatened the Pharaoh, he led his people out into the desert, and so on. It is by virtue of these particular actions and their special significance in the overall development of events that we can make the more sweeping claim about rescuing the Hebrew people.

Is it possible, however, to say more specifically what God does in rescuing the Hebrew people from Egypt? The content of the answer to this question will depend upon the general view one takes of God's activity in relation to nature, humankind, and history. Most contemporary theologians are disinclined to identify God's activity with a series of miraculous events, even though this would provide a relatively simple base from which to identify God. A theologian may not want to rule out the possibility of such events, but he is unlikely to give them a central place in his understanding of, say, the Exodus story.

If God's actions are not particular miraculous events, then in what sense is God an agent in the events of the Hebrews' liberation?[21] One might answer that God is at work in historical events in a variety of ways more subtle than the production of plagues and pillars of fire. Theological and devotional traditions also speak of God "working upon the human heart," inspiring persons with an awareness of the divine presence and power, giving courage and hope where there was anxiety and despair, calling human freedom into the realization of new possibilities. One might argue that God shapes the direction of human history (and its natural foundations) without simply overruling creaturely agencies in spectacular displays of sovereign power. I am not concerned here with the complex issues that would be raised by an attempt to develop these suggestions into a unified interpretation of talk about divine action.[22] Rather, the point is that actions of this sort *cannot be easily identified* as a basis for the identification of God as their agent. They are not readily observable as events in nature and human history. If God's actions are understood in these more subtle ways, it becomes very difficult to point to a discrete event and say, "There, by 'God' I mean the agent of that event." This will be true even if one argues that at certain points God makes his action known to man in a special way, so that these events are preeminently the acts of God in which his nature and his intention in human history are disclosed.

How then are we to identify God as an agent of intentional actions? Whatever the particular content of our claims about God's acts, our reference to them will involve "telling a story" that ties events together in a meaningful pattern and relates this pattern to the purposive activity of God.[23] The starting point of our reference to the divine agent and his acts will lie in accessible events within our spatio-temporal world, but these events provide the basis for reference to God only when taken up and given a place within an account of God's active relation to our world. Identification of God as a unique subject of speech involves a whole network of claims about the nature of God, the openness of human history and nature to God's influence, God's dealings with us in the past and his purposes for our future, and so on. The effect of this theistic story is to superimpose a pattern of divine intention on the events of human history. It weaves these events together into a meaningful sequence, the central theme of which is the working out of God's purposes in relation to humankind. In doing so, the story suggests that we acknowledge a level of significance in events that would not otherwise enter our description of them.

God, therefore, is identified as an actor introduced within a story. But this story (which may become quite complex once a philosopher or theologian gets ahold of it) is not left as a piece of elaborate fantasy. Rather, it purports to be the story of our lives and our history. The setting of the story is continuous with the world within which the rest of our references are made, and the events it narrates coincide with events we can identify in our shared field of reference. Here story-relative identification has been tied into our shared field of reference. We can say that this kind of identification is *story-bound* rather than *story-relative*. Reference to God is story-bound insofar as it is dependent upon a network of supporting claims that, taken as a whole, set the context within which we can identify God. Reference to God is not story-relative, however, because the theistic story is not left as an isolated world of its own, disconnected from the rest of our references. On the contrary, the story we tell about God as an agent of intentional actions not only introduces God as a subject of reference but also provides individuating relations that connect God to the events and individuals that populate our world. The theistic story seeks to broaden and complete our field of reference by describing the ultimate context in which we live our lives. In order to do so, it takes up within itself the whole field of references in which we ourselves have a place. Far from being isolated from the rest of our references, this story embraces as many of them as it can, relating them all to the central referent of the story: God.

It is certainly possible to challenge the plausibility of the theist's story. There are any number of alternative stories that might be told about the events of our shared history. St. Augustine, for example, lived for many years within the grip of a Manichaean story that placed the events of human life in the context of a battle between opposing powers of good and evil, light and darkness. The process by which that story lost plausibility and was replaced by a Christian (and Neoplatonic) story is complex enough to provide material for a great autobiography. There is certainly no simple way to certify the truth of the story he adopted or demonstrate the error of the story he left behind, but however difficult it may be to determine whether the theist's story is the right one to tell about our experience, it remains the case that within the context provided by that story it is possible to refer to God and his actions. Note that one does not simply affirm or reject isolated references to God; rather, one affirms or rejects a whole network of beliefs that together provide the setting for reference to God. That is to say, one adopts or rejects the whole of the theist's story rather than just a single proposition about God.

It is important to recognize that the identification of God is not the only reference we make that is story-bound. We do, after all, tell a story about ourselves as agents and about certain of our behaviors as actions. We do not identify agents on the basis of a neutral-event description; rather, we identify an agent from his behavior taken as intentional action. Act description and agent identification are a logically inseparable pair. Taken together they represent a possible description of our experience: one that is systematically tied into our identification of objects in time and space but that is *not* reducible to such identifications.[24]

I want to comment briefly on a second set of problems. We need to ask whether there are limits upon the effectiveness of the act-agent relation as an individuating relation. Does this relation in every case pick out a single subject of reference? The answer to this question, I think, is No. Some acts can have more than one agent, or, to put it more precisely, a single act description (e.g., ringing the bell) may be exemplified by two agents simultaneously in a single identifiable event (e.g., the bell ringing). If we refer to "the person who is ringing the bell," we will not in every case be referring to just one individual: there may be more than one person's hands on the bell rope. To identify an event and refer it to an agent as his act may not be sufficient as an identifying reference. Under what conditions *will* the act-agent relation be sufficient?

First, the act-agent relation will successfully individuate if there are circumstantial considerations that rule out ascribing a single instance of a particular action to more than one agent. Reference to "the person who is ringing the bell" will effectively identify a single individual if we know, for example, that the bell-ringing apparatus is constructed in such a way that only one person could ring it. In general, a particular action can be used to pick out a single individual as its agent if there are features of the context of action or characteristics of the agent that eliminate the possibility that any other agent could perform that particular action.

Are there circumstantial considerations that allow us to make an individuating reference to God on the basis of his actions? If we operate within the terms of the theistic story, then there are such considerations. The story that has been developed by the dominant theological tradition is stubbornly monotheistic. It establishes a context within which God's powers of action are unique, and systematically rules out the possibility of the actions ascribed to God being ascribed to any other agent. Does this simply beg the question? It does if one refuses to acknowledge that identification of God and his actions is dependent upon a larger theistic story that introduces a set of conditions that make these identifications possible. This is not to say that these identifications are story-relative in the strong sense. The theistic story includes references to events that belong to our shared spatio-temporal frame of reference. Nonetheless, the theist's reference to God will be adequately individuating only within the context provided by his story.

The monotheism of the story is not simply the result of circumstantial stipulation, however. Theists have typically insisted that there can in principle be only one agent who acts as God acts. This points to a second way in which the act-agent relation can be uniquely individuating: an action can be used as the basis for identifying an agent if that action admits of ascription to only one agent, whatever the special circumstantial considerations. We might call these cases "logically individuating actions." They will be easily translatable into logically individuating descriptions, and perhaps could be considered a sub-set of such descriptions. We might, for example, use the action description "running faster than any other human being" to pick out the single individual to whom this action can be ascribed. This action description includes as part of its content a specification of the type of agent to which reference is being made (a human being), and so supposes a network of supporting references. This need not be the case, however. The theist might refer to the agent who, through his intentional action, brings into existence all beings other than himself. While this action could in principle be performed by only one individual, the action description itself does not give us any information about this agent beyond ascribing a crucial (and very unusual) action to him. This identification shares the descriptive incompleteness of logically individuating descriptions. It makes an unambiguous reference, but leaves us largely in the dark about the individual to whom reference is being made.

There are, of course, certain special difficulties associated with this traditional theistic reference. Not only does the individual identified as the agent of this action remain elusive, but the action used to make the identification is inevitably opaque to us. The function or effect attributed to this action is clear enough: if this agent did not do whatever he does in creating other beings there would be no beings other than himself. But the particular nature of this action is inevitably obscure to us: we cannot say more exactly what this agent does in "bringing into being. . . ." The action at which this phrase hints is hardly a familiar feature of our own lives as agents. If one refers at all to this unique action, one does so within the context of the larger story that theists tell about human beings and our world.[25] One can, of course, reject the theist's story and refuse to view humankind and nature as radically dependent upon a single creative agent; the point here is not that one ought to take up this theistic view, but rather that if one does, then one has available a logically individuating action description by which to identify God. Once again, this identification is story-bound without being story-relative.

There is a third case in which an action description can be used to identify an agent uniquely. It appears that any single instance of a *basic* action (i.e., an action without instrumental substructure) can in principle be ascribed to only one agent. Returning to the example used above, a single instance of the action described as "ringing the bell" might be ascribed simultaneously to more than one agent, but a single instance of the action described as "moving arms up and down" or "grasping the rope" could not be ascribed to more than one agent *if* these are basic actions. If a behavior that is within my repertoire of basic actions is produced in me by another agent, then it is not (in this instance) an intentional action of mine at all.[26] As long as there is an instrumental substructure to action, however, it will often be possible for two agents to be involved in bringing about a single outcome that can simultaneously be ascribed to each as his action.[27]

Are any of the actions the theist ascribes to God basic actions for God? This will be a difficult question to answer because it very quickly becomes impossible to analyze the substructure of actions attributed to God. In the examples discussed above, the action of "rescuing the Hebrew people" clearly has an instrumental substructure of some kind. Depending on one's theological inclinations, one might see this action as the outcome of intentionally prior actions such as "sending plagues" and "parting the Red Sea" or of actions such as "inspiring Moses," "evoking awareness of the divine presence and power," "giving courage and hope to the people," and so on. It is difficult to know whether one should say that any of these actions is basic for God. But we need not pursue this question here. The identification of these actions is dependent upon the story the theist tells about historical events, and the decision that any one of them constitutes a basic action for God is dependent upon the particular way in which a theologian develops the theistic story—that is, the identification of God's basic actions is a matter of detail within a specific theological proposal. It is enough for us to note that the identification of God from an event taken as his basic action will, once again, be story-bound.

CONCLUSION

Perhaps enough has been said to indicate the possibilities and problems that will arise for an attempt to identify God as an agent who cannot be "placed" spatially. Such an agent can be identified as a referent of human speech, but that reference takes place within a theistic story that includes but goes beyond the particulars of our ordinary network of references. The story we tell about God as an agent of intentional actions sets him in a unique relation to events within our shared field of experience. It may be difficult to state truth conditions for this story, but if one operates within the context it establishes, then individuating reference to God is possible.

The considerations that Strawson introduces in making a case against mind-body dualism, therefore, need not lead us to give up the possibility of conceiving of God as a personal agent who is not a person. Strawson's argument, in concert with those considered in

Chapter 3, may prompt us to reject the dualist's radical distinction between mind and body in the human agent. But none of these arguments yields the conclusion that being a body is a necessary condition for being an agent.

The option is still open to conceive of God as a nonbodily agent, but it remains to be seen how we might actually do so and whether there are further problems to deal with along the way. In giving up dualism, we give up appeal to the human mind as a readily available model of an agent who is inherently nonbodily (even if associated with a body). The criticisms of mind-body dualism that we have considered point beyond their negative polemics to the project of conceiving of the human being as a unified individual who is both agent and organism: an individual whose unity cannot be broken down into two more basic unities. We need to ask whether this way of thinking about persons as agents can be helpful in structuring reflection upon God as an agent. If we reject mind-body dualism, can we any longer extract theologically useful analogies from our concept of the human agent? In attempting to use *this* concept of an agent in theology, must we modify it so profoundly that it finally breaks down altogether?

Once again, discussion will move through two stages. First, I will sketch out an account of the human agent understood not as a combination of two simple substances, but rather as a psychophysical unit. So far the concept of a psychophysical unit has been treated only formally (e.g., as the idea of a single subject of both M-predicates and P-predicates) and so remains merely an appealing abstraction. We need to see more concretely what it means to say that the human agent is a single unified center of both bodily life and personal action. Second, I will go on to examine whether and how this account of the human agent might provide conceptual structures upon which we can draw in conceiving of the divine agent.

PART THREE

Persons and the Divine Agent

CHAPTER 5

Persons as Agents

1. THE BODILY AGENT AS A PSYCHOPHYSICAL UNIT

If dualism is rejected, how are we to understand the bodily agent? We can no longer think of the agent as a special entity joined to the body. It is potentially misleading, therefore, to speak of the human agent as "having a body," as though an agent possesses a body in roughly the same sense that a person possesses a suit of clothes: it is something that could be done without, but it makes social life less complicated. We can say that the agent *is* his body, though this will be incorrect if taken as saying that the agent is "nothing but" a body. An agent cannot be a mere body, that is, a physical entity or organism to which no intentional action (or, more generally, no "P-predicate" whatsoever) can be ascribed. But neither is the agent something that is added to a body. It is least misleading, if a bit awkward, to say that some bodies (physical organisms) are agents. A body is an agent by virtue of operating intentionally, and therefore consciously, in at least a small range of its activities.

Note that consciousness is ascribed here as a characteristic of the way the agent operates, not as the name of a special entity which *is* the agent. We speak of a conscious regulation of behavior rather than of a regulation of behavior by consciousness. Since an agent must be conscious of his actions (though not necessarily conscious of every correct description of his intentions), an agent who is a body will not be merely a physical entity but rather a psychophysical unity. The bodily agent will be a psychophysical unit capable of intentionally modifying some of the processes that constitute its own life.

The mind-body dualist might complain that this does nothing to explain the capacity of persons to operate as agents in undertaking intentional actions. I have already (in Chap. 3) commented on the failure of the dualist's own proposal, for all its apparent simplicity, to shed light on this question, but the question is evidently a legitimate one. How is the psychophysical agent able to regulate those stretches of his activity that are involved in his intentional actions? It appears that any fully developed theory of action will have to address this question. But it is wisest here, given the particular interests with which I am approaching the concept of the psychophysical agent, to note the question without offering any detailed proposal. Much of what the philosopher has to say about the "mechanisms" of the agent's intentional regulation of bodily action will bear upon questions about the relation of consciousness and its physical basis, and therefore upon neurophysiological information that is itself quite sketchy. The philosopher can map out conceptual possibilities, but these will be characterized as much by imaginative penetration as by solid information.

I wish, then, to consider the concept of a psychophysical agent on a level that is relatively neutral with regard to any particular explanatory proposal about the agent's intentional control of action. There are two points argued in the preceding chapters from which we can take our bearings. First, whatever theory is offered to account for the agent's capacity to regulate his actions, that capacity must be acknowledged if we are to speak of an agent at all. Second, given the results of our discussion of mind-body dualism, this capacity for intentional action will be exercised by the psychophysical unit, and not by a special entity distinct from but conjoined to the body. If both of these points are granted, then we can develop a concept of the psychophysical agent without venturing any detailed explanation of the agent's capacity to act intentionally.[1]

In the discussion that follows we will focus first upon the role of bodily life in providing the basis and medium for the agent's intentional actions, and then consider the emergence of the agent's distinctive personal identity in and through his intentional activity. This approach should bring an overall picture of the psychophysical agent into focus and shed light on those conceptual structures that are most relevant to assessing the possibilities for conceiving of God as an agent.

2. BASIC ACTIONS

If we are to understand the role played by the body in providing the basis for a person's operation as agent, it will be helpful to develop briefly the idea of a basic action, introduced in Chapter 2. I noted there that the instrumental substructure of any complex action must at some point come to an end. Returning to an example already used, if the cook is to call people to dinner, he may have to ring a bell. If he is to ring the bell, he may have to pull a rope. And if he is to pull the rope, he will have to move his hands and arms in certain ways. This regress can only come to an end in an action that he undertakes without having to do anything else in order to act as he intends. This will be a basic action. Basic actions are intentionally simple; that is, they have no instrumental substructure. But they will often have an instrumental superstructure; that is, they will lie at the base of complex action sequences in which we do one thing (e.g., ring the bell) in order to bring about another (e.g., call people to dinner). We can speak, therefore, of an agent's regulation of basic actions as "direct" in contrast to his "indirect" control of the outcome of an instrumentally complex action, since an agent does not need to employ any instrumental means in order to undertake a basic action. We might say, using a bit of philosophically suspect ordinary language, that he can simply undertake the action "at will."

The dualist and nondualist alike must ground the instrumental substructure of every complex action in a basic action. We have seen that the dualist who subscribes to a volition theory extends the instrumental substructure of bodily action back into mental acts of will. On the volition theory, no bodily action can be a basic action, since bodily actions are always the outcome of some causally prior mental act performed in order to bring about that bodily movement. All basic actions must, on this account, be mental acts of will. When dualism is rejected, the instrumental substructure of a complex bodily action can end in an intentionally simple bodily action—that is, in a bodily action undertaken without the agent first having to perform any other intentional action, either another bodily action or an intentional mental act. A basic bodily action will have the same function in an instrumental action series as the dualist's mental act of will. It will be performed intentionally, and yet will not be the outcome of any prior intentional action.

The concept of a basic action needs a good deal of development beyond these rather formal remarks. It is not immediately apparent which actions one should identify as basic actions. In the case of the bell ringer, we clearly will not treat "calling people to dinner," "ringing the bell," or "pulling the rope" as basic actions. Each of these is performed only by undertaking certain prerequisite actions. What of the movement of the bell ringer's hands and arms? Is this his basic action? His bodily movements, of course, involve complex physiological processes in his nervous system, muscles and so on. If he is to move his arms, the appropriate muscles must contract, and those muscle contractions are finally dependent (we may suppose) upon certain processes in the brain. Must we pursue the agent's basic action back into the minutiae of neurophysiological process? Are we to identify some particular point in this neurophysiological chain as the agent's basic action—perhaps an originating event (insofar as this claim could be made for any particular event or limited set of events) in the brain? This would be an odd move. For the agent will not be aware of the neurophysiological detail of his action, and in any case does not need to attend to it. His intention is to perform behavior of a description such as "moving my arms so as to grasp the rope." The bell ringer would be nonplussed if told that his project included "engaging certain neurophysiological processes in order to cause some fifty different muscles to contract with proper synchronization." We may want to say that this describes something the person does—after all, these physiological events are more than something he passively suffers; they do not merely happen to him, but are performed by him in performing the intentional action that involves them. But on the other hand, the agent does not attend to these processes as a distinct sub-action performed with the further purpose of moving his hands and arms. He does not enact neurophysiological processes as the *means* of carrying through the bodily action of grasping the rope; rather, he undertakes the action of grasping, with all of its "hidden" neurophysiological detail, as a unit without intentional substructure.

The unit of activity, then, that is subject to the agent's intentional regulation under normal conditions (e.g., when there is no physical impairment) appears to be the whole set of processes involved in raising his arm. The agent does not need to attend to the causal connections of the sequence of neurophysiological processes involved in a basic bodily action; he need only set these processes to work as a whole, regulating their overall effect (e.g., an arm movement of a particular duration, velocity, direction, etc.). In the action of ringing the bell, the agent does not intentionally stimulate certain neurological structures in order to produce the movement of his arms, but he does intentionally move his arms in order to pull the bell rope.

This is not to say that the agent always or even very often contemplates a basic bodily action as a well-articulated sub-act within an instrumental action sequence. He is more likely to intend, without filling in much detail, whatever general bodily movement might be expected to bring about the end sought in his action. In fact, an agent's attention may sometimes be only marginally focused upon his bodily movements. A golfer's attention may reside with the ball and club, while his bodily action (if all goes well) brings about the relation he intends between them. But an agent *can* attend to the particulars of his bodily action if need be. The golfer can focus his attention upon the rhythm of his swing, the position of his feet, the flex of his wrists, and so on. He cannot, however, improve his accuracy with a golf club by attending to the initiation of neurological sequences in his brain. The neurophysiological detail of bodily movement remains submerged for the agent in the overt bodily action he intends.

These observations on the individuation of basic bodily actions could bear further refinement. Enough has been said, however, to give a rough indication of which among the various descriptions of the events involved in bodily actions are to be identified as descriptions of basic actions. Descriptions that identify basic bodily actions will pick out stretches of bodily activity intended as units without internal intentional complexity (e.g., raising and lowering one's arms, turning one's head, making a fist, working one's fingers, etc.). Descriptions of intentionally complex bodily actions, on the other hand, will involve reference to the outcome (outcome$_2$) generated by basic bodily actions (e.g., raising my right arm by lifting it with my left, ringing a bell, turning on a light, casting a vote, etc.). Basic bodily actions are not to be identified with any particular moment (including an originating event, if one could be picked out) in the causal sequence of organic processes at work in a bodily movement. Rather, a basic bodily action marks out a sequence of bodily processes undertaken as a unit defined by the agent's intention for the overall effect of those processes.

3. THE BODILY BASIS OF INTENTIONAL ACTION

The Body as Ground and Limit of the Agent's Capacity to Act. An agent's repertoire of basic bodily actions will vary with the structure and condition of the organism that bears his life. The particular form that bodily life takes for human beings as a species and for each of us as individuals determines a range of possible actions we can initiate. Our capacity to act intentionally is rooted in biological processes that are finally inaccessible to our direct regulation (that is, to regulation in any basic action).[2] The processes of organic life maintain their dynamic equilibrium automatically. They need not, and indeed cannot, be continuously enacted by the person whose life they maintain. These subintentional processes of bodily life, however, constitute causally necessary conditions for bodily actions. There must be living muscle tissue, healthy nerve networks, properly formed bones, and so forth if I am to perform the basic action of raising my arm. I do not enact these stable patterns of biological process. They are simply given for me. Yet these biological processes, inaccessible to direct intentional regulation, provide the dependable structures that are put to work in intentional action.

I will leave to the physiologist questions about specifically how automatic bodily processes provide the foundation for intentional bodily action. An abstract conceptual picture that is perhaps not too wide of the mark might locate the subintentional bodily basis of intentional action in networks of balanced organic processes that are subject to systemic modifications corresponding to bodily actions. The subintentional processes of bodily life, that is, establish stable structures of organic activity that permit a margin of intentional variation. The scope of such variation is limited, however, by the capacity of these structures to maintain their function in the face of modification. My capacity to intentionally move my arms, for example, is dependent upon an appropriate variability in the stable structures of organic process that constitute bodily life. In raising my arms in the air, those processes are set to work in the particular pattern that constitutes that bodily movement, but the modification of these processes is limited by the need to maintain their integrity. I can only lift so much weight and hold it for so long. If I push too hard at these limits, the bodily capacity for that action will break down (e.g., the muscles will lose their capacity to flex and I will drop the weight). Precisely as stable processes that permit variation, the given patterns of bodily life provide a restricted set of possibilities for action. The agent does not choose and enact these basic patterns of bodily life; he can choose and enact only particular variations of those processes.

Our intentional activity as agents appears, then, as an embellishment along the margins of the automatism of bodily processes. Our "charter of action" is biologically stated. But the range of basic actions of which an agent is capable is not precisely fixed and utterly immune to modification. A great deal of human satisfaction and human distress is associated with the fact that capacities for basic actions can be acquired and lost. The victim of illness or accident may lose the capacity to perform a whole range of bodily movements as basic actions. When paralyzed, a limb that the agent had formerly experienced as a ready set of capacities for engaging his world becomes dumb flesh, strangely alien and thing-like. Movement of that limb is now possible only as the outcome of an intentionally prior action, as when it is lifted by the agent's "good" arm. If a person is fortunate enough to regain the use of an immobilized limb, he virtually reclaims it as part of his effective self.

We are perpetually occupied in extending and refining our capacity to regulate our bodily actions. A pianist once described to me the long struggle she had gone through to strengthen the weaker fingers of each hand, speed up the movement of her thumbs, and then refine these skills so that she could regulate her touch at the keyboard. The development of such special physical skills is not only a crucial part of many people's work, it is also one of the most familiar ways in which we entertain ourselves. A child enjoys the uncertainties of trying to maintain his balance while walking on a narrow curb. He may grow up to spend his free time seeking out new challenges to his capacity to stay upright on skis. The satisfaction of such activities lies not only in the exercise of an acquired skill, but also in trying out that skill in new situations that put it to the test and provide an opportunity for its further refinement. We find it intrinsically satisfying to extend the range of physical performances subject to our intentional regulation as basic actions.

It appears that the scope of a person's intentional regulation of bodily action is itself subject to a degree of intentional regulation. Persons can intentionally expand their repertoire of basic bodily actions, though the action of developing a new physical skill will never itself be a basic action.[3] The capacity of any human being to expand the range and refine the detail of bodily action will be limited, however, by the very patterns of organic activity that permit him his life as agent. There is always this two-sidedness to our experience of bodily agency; our bodiliness both establishes a capacity for intentional action and limits the versatility of our active existence. For us, the possibility of intentional action is given together with its limitations.

It is no small task, as we explore our capacities as agents, to come to terms with the brute givenness, the opacity to intentional control, of the defining conditions of our lives as agents. The givenness of our capacities as bodily agents no doubt contributes to the feeling of being at odds with the body; we sometimes experience the body as an entity over against us and resistant to us (that is, to our interests and intentions). Human beings have rarely been very comfortable with their restricted charter of action. We aspire beyond our particular limitations and envision other structures of life and action. It is little wonder that a figure like Proteus, free to modify the form of his agency, captures the human imagination.

We cannot fully affirm those powers of action that we do possess, however, without acknowledging that our capacity to determine what shape our lives will take is limited in certain characteristic ways that help define what we are. Our powers of action are rooted in the given capacities and tied to the rhythmic needs of bodily life. The biological basis of our operation as agents finally imposes outside limits on the possibilities for intentionally simple bodily action. But if our versatility as agents of basic actions is inevitably limited, the scope of our activity is expanded indefinitely by our capacity to recognize and exploit instrumental connections (e.g., the causal regularities described by the natural sciences). We develop the range of our activity beyond our biological limits by putting our capacity for basic action to work in intentionally complex actions that indirectly bring about what we intend. In this way our repertoire of basic bodily actions becomes the foundation for an endless variety of projects and an indefinite range of aspiration.

The Integration of Bodily Automatism and Intentional Action. This account of the psychophysical agent pictures bodily life as providing a stable structure of activity within which intentional action appears as a dependent and marginal variation.[4] The agent is a smoothly integrated complex of activity in which intentional action emerges all but imperceptibly out of its base in the subintentional processes of bodily life. It would be very difficult to say at what point organic reactivity is subsumed by intentional action or just where unreflective intentional action slips back into bodily automatism. I feel an itch and I move to scratch it, though I may hardly be aware of doing so. Perhaps head scratching becomes a mannerism for me, something I do on certain occasions whether or not there is an itch—whenever someone asks a difficult question, say. If such behaviors are intentional action, they are certainly an inarticulate and unselfconscious form of it. And if such behaviors are not intentional action, they at least could very easily become such. The point here is not to decide just what should be said about cases such as these, but rather to suggest that our activity as agents is quite subtly built up out of the organic responsiveness of bodily life.

Certainly many if not most of our intentional actions are largely unreflective. Our interest is "caught" by an apparent possibility for action and we act, without the transition from perceived possibility to enacted project being interrupted by an examination of alternatives or a consideration of consequences not immediately apparent.[5] We most often recognize and discriminate among possibilities for action at a level of uncritical engagement with our field of action. The possibility of explicitly seeking out and examining alternate action possibilities is latent here, submerged in our immediate interaction with our world. The standard case of intentional action, the enactment of a well-formed and carefully evaluated project, is surely the exception rather than the rule in our activity as agents from moment to moment. In any case, there is a range in the degree to which we are self-conscious, critical, and deliberate in intentional action, a range that at its lower end trails off into behavior in which purpose recedes into mere functionality and action disappears into organic response.

Even as intentional action becomes clearly distinguishable from bodily automatism, it remains smoothly integrated with the subintentional processes that ground it. Note, for example, the way in which intentional action may be woven around patterns of bodily behavior in which intentionality in any full sense has not yet appeared. I slam on the brakes of my car when a child darts into the street. My initial reaction to this sudden turn of events is very close to a mere "startle reaction," an automatic bodily reflex in response to a sudden stimulus. But my reaction is not dysfunctional (indeed "aimless") as is, for example, the convulsive jump that the child might provoke from me (to his great delight) by leaping from around a corner and shouting "Boo!" My initial reaction to the child's presence in the street both takes place in a broader context of intentional activity (driving the car) and represents a first crucial step toward carrying out that activity successfully. It is as if behavior that begins as a virtually automatic reaction (slamming on the brakes) is subsumed by my regulative intention (to avoid hitting the child) as soon as my ability to assess the situation "catches up" with my immediate reaction. My action of avoiding the child is dependent upon my first reaction, and if I were not confident of that reaction I would have no business driving a car. In fact, my immediate reaction may well be a *trained* response. I may have carefully prepared myself for situations like this one by practicing emergency maneuvers when learning to drive a car. In that case, I have intentionally developed certain specific reactions in order to ensure a reliable start on action intended for circumstances that develop suddenly. It is as if the creatures of Pavlov's experiments were to begin intentionally conditioning themselves so as to develop responses that serve their purposes. This is a key element in a great many skilled physical activities, from driving an automobile to trapshooting.

The Bodily Orientation of Intentional Action. Not only is our activity as agents smoothly integrated with its bodily basis, but it also receives an initial orientation from the demands of bodily life. The rhythms of bodily life establish an agenda for action that cannot be ignored without risking our capacity to act at all. We have noted that the ability to act intentionally is dependent upon subintentional biological processes. At the same time we must note that the continued functioning of those subintentional processes is in certain respects dependent upon our intentional activity: we must keep ourselves fueled with nutrients that maintain organic life, respond to changes in our surroundings that threaten our comfort or health, and understand the natural environment of our action well enough to meet these needs successfully. Beyond bare survival needs, there are biologically established drives to exercise the powers and experience the satisfactions of which we are capable (e.g., the array of satisfactions that Freud associates with the erotic instinct).

It has become the business of psychoanalytic theory to chart the geography of human desires and to reflect upon the dynamics of their expression (both overt and indirect) in the variegated universe of human behavior. We do not need the sophistication of psychoanalytic theory, however, to make our point here. The capacity to act intentionally has a biological function, namely, to meet the needs and satisfy the vital drives of the agent organism. Given along with the capacity for action is an orientation of interest, a complex set of dispositions to act. Just as the agent finds himself with a given capacity for action, so he finds himself identified with a biologically established array of vital interests. Concern for the vital interests of bodily life is a central, even foundational, theme in our intentional actions.[6]

No claim is being made here that all human activity can be adequately "explained" by appeal to its biological roots or that all of the interests at work in an agent's active life can be reduced to "instinctual" drives rooted in bodily life. Rather, I am suggesting that no matter how far our interests may range beyond the immediate demands of bodily life, human action is always bound to and woven around a biological agenda. The agenda for action rooted in bodily life is clearly not so uniform from individual to individual nor so detailed in its demands as to rule out all significant variation in the pattern of individual lives and the form of human communities. Just as subintentional bodily processes allow for a range of variation in intentional action, so the demands of those biological processes for maintenance allow a broad range of variation in the particulars of their satisfaction. The body requires nourishment, its organic fuel. But it does not require that its protein come in the form of filet mignon covered with a Bordelaise sauce. Those details are left to the invention of the agent and his culture. As persons engage their world and work out forms of personal and social life, they develop their biologically established interests into uniquely human activities that reveal the distinctive capacities of human existence. Needs for nourishment and shelter are expanded into the distinctive cuisine and architecture of a particular culture. The need to secure the means of life is elaborated into forms of social cooperation and control, into an economic and political system. The need to know what in our natural environment sustains us and what threatens us is subsumed within a larger drive to understand the workings of nature. In short, the vital interests of bodily life are focused and developed in a shared culture that becomes an interest in itself and reacts back upon the basic bodily interests that are expressed within it.

I do not want to stray too far into this amateur cultural anthropology. The principal points to be made here can be put succinctly. First, a person's active life as agent receives a continuing orientation from its bodily basis. Second, the requirements of bodily life do not in every case specify their objects with precision nor dictate the means by which those objects are secured. Third, our interests develop beyond direct biological utility. We may even come to act against the biological basis of our existence as agents—although in this respect the given limitations of our lives as agents are evident, since obviously one can act against one's vital bodily interests only at the cost of endangering one's capacity to act at all. Hence a fourth point: though our interests may range far beyond the immediate needs and drives of bodily life, our projects must be accommodated to its rhythms.

4. INTENTIONAL ACTION AND PERSONAL IDENTITY[7]

Our lives as agents, then, remain firmly rooted in bodily life. Indeed, it is not too much to say that the life of the body *is* the agent's life—but the life of the body is the life of an agent only because the processes that constitute bodily life admit a range of intentional variation in basic actions. Given this capacity for intentional action, that which is distinctively personal about persons can appear. In the exercise of our capacity for intentional action we both become and make known who we are. As a person puts his capacities for action to work in meeting and moving beyond the basic demands of bodily life, he develops his own unique identity as an agent. He emerges as a distinctive individual both for himself and for others as he works out his purposes in interaction with his natural and social worlds.

An agent's personal identity appears in the complex continuity and interconnectedness of his acts. If we seek to understand *who* an individual is in any very significant sense, we must look to his characteristic interests, his typical responses to situations, his special capacities, his distinctive style, his inveterate habits, his most firmly held policies, his darkest regrets. We must, that is, consider how he conducts his life, and we must identify the most significant patterns that appear over the course of his activity. We cannot avoid regarding an agent historically: we turn to his past in trying to grasp who he is now and in forming expectations about who he will become. This is a difficult task. We may in the process discover considerable diversity, marked change, perhaps apparent contradiction. There is a certain inexhaustibility about the identity of an agent; no simple description will do him justice. And it is noteworthy that the difficulty of offering a penetrating analysis of the most significant patterns of action in an agent's life is usually compounded, not lessened, when the person one is seeking to understand is oneself.

Continuities of Project and of Character. The continuity and interconnection we look for in seeking to understand the identity of any agent, including ourselves, will appear most simply in patterns of descriptively similar projects that appear over the course of an agent's activity. These continuities in the intentional content of action, or continuities of project, will appear wherever actions of a similar description are undertaken with a significant regularity. We identify continuities of project, for example, when we say that someone is an inveterate tax evader and a dabbler in politics (these being two of his enduring interests), a heavy drinker and fast driver (these being two of his less commendable habits), a regular participant in the activities of his church and the Chamber of Commerce (this being among his established policies).

On this level continuities of project are quite unproblematic and easily identified. The person who has these interests, habits, and policies is likely to be aware of them. His consciously adopted policies of action, in fact, will represent continuities of project that he explicitly intends. But there are other less obvious and sometimes more illuminating continuities that can be identified in an agent's actions—continuities that may not be immediately apparent either to the agent or to others. As I noted in Chapter 2, actions often belong to complex and extended instrumental-action sequences—that is, an action of one description may be undertaken in order to achieve some further purpose, and so can usually be redescribed in terms of that further intention. As a result, a number of actions of which quite different descriptions have been given can sometimes be redescribed in terms of an identical or analogous further purpose at work in each. Actions that are apparently unrelated can in this way be seen as different instances of action of a similar description. A significant continuity of project then emerges where before we had identified only a number of quite different particular undertakings. This vastly complicates the identification of continuities of project.

The further purposes of our actions often go unstated and are sometimes unrecognized. In this connection, an agent can be said to be unaware of certain of his intentions, and yet it may be that a knowledge of these unexpressed further intentions would enable us to recognize significant continuities in his actions. Further, even if an agent's intentions in action could be stated without any unarticulated residue, it remains the case that an agent will be unaware of many of the continuities of project that might be identified in his actions, for while a continuity of project represents a coherent pattern in what an agent intends, this pattern itself is not very often intended. An agent, that is, does not generally make it his project to display the continuous themes that appear in his actions (though he does do this when he adopts a life-style, a moral rule, or any policy of action). Unintended patterns of intentional action, however, can easily go unrecognized.

In trying to undertstand the distinctive personal identity of an agent, we not only look for continuities in the intentional content of his projects but also for continuities in the character of those projects, which is to say, in the evaluations that might be offered of his actions. We not only note that an individual is, say, an inveterate tax evader (a continuity of project) but also comment on his dishonesty and greed. I will call patterns of the latter sort *continuities of character.* [8] In Chapter 1 I discussed the class of terms used in evaluating an agent's actions and in commenting on his character. Character trait predicates do not indicate that an agent typically undertakes actions of a specific description (as does the ascription of a continuity of project); rather, the ascription of a trait of character calls attention to a pattern of actions that, though perhaps quite different and unconnected in their particular intentions, suggest and warrant a general evaluation. If I am told that John is a very cautious fellow, I am not given any specific information about what he will do; I am, however, alerted to a characteristic style of action that may appear in a number of very different projects. He may counsel a friend to marry, divest himself of stock, order a steak for lunch, and in all these actions be methodical, deliberate, and wary of error.

The diversity of actions that can be called upon to support the ascription of a particular trait of character is vast. As I argued in Chapter 1, there is an indefinite variety of actions that can be evaluated as wise or generous or aggressive or the like. Further, the number of possible associations of an agent's actions into patterns suggestive of distinctive character traits is also vast. Depending upon how we associate and weigh an array of actions, an agent may appear either malicious or merely thoughtless, wise or merely shrewd. As a result, the recognition of continuities of character is sometimes difficult and arguable. In suggesting that a person exemplifies a particular trait of character, we may be pointing to a pattern in his actions that is quite subtle and complex. The agent himself may well have little or no idea that his actions can be seen in this light. It is notoriously true that there is no first-person advantage in the assessment of character. I must struggle as much or more to arrive at a perceptive estimate of my own character as to appreciate that of another.

The Motivational Background of Action. Our interest in trying to understand the personal identity of an agent is not exhausted by noting continuities in the content and character of his actions. We are also interested in the memories and perceptions of the past, attitudes and beliefs, moods and emotions, and bodily needs and drives that form the context out of which the agent acts. Here our concern is directed to the diverse array of factors at work in giving shape to an agent's conduct. If in pointing to continuities of project we identify an agent's characteristic intentions, here we seek to understand the various influences and considerations that lead him to those intentions—the *motivational background* of action.[9] This motivational context will clearly be quite complex, sending its roots down into the deeply buried sediment of past experience and reaching out into the matrix of social relations in which the agent is situated. I have already indicated something of the role the body plays in contributing recurrent themes of interest to the motivational background of action. My purpose at this point is simply to acknowledge our interest in a variety of factors at work in the background of action and to indicate something of the role this background plays in giving shape to the agent's distinctive personal identity.

An agent's activity in recognizing and pursuing possibilities for action involves a dynamic integration of his encounter with his immediate field of interaction (his natural and social world), his past experience and action, the rhythmic needs and drives of bodily life, and the affective intonations that all of these bear. The convergence of all these factors forms the context within which possibilities for action are perceived and the agent's energies selectively poured into his various projects. We might say that an agent lives at the point of intersection between his field of interaction, with all its demands and possibilities, and the array of mnemonic, affective, and physiological factors that constitute the present subjective context of action. An agent acts from and within this complex setting, and his action represents the drawing together of these various factors in an intention for the shape of his activity in the future.

The interaction of the elements at work in the background of an agent's actions is extraordinarily complex. It is important to note that the process of their integration in the emergence of the agent's intentions is not, on every level, equally accessible to reflection and criticism. Particular elements within the background of action may become the object of critical scrutiny and intentional modification. An agent may make it his project to review his past conduct, to criticize his beliefs, to analyze his emotions, or to challenge his social roles. But there are limits upon our ability to be critically self-conscious about the motivational context from which we act. We do, after all, inhabit a complex affective, mnemonic, and attitudinal setting in the very act of critical self-examination. Our immediate conscious-intentional activity always remains a step ahead of reflective self-examination. Projects "occur" to us, and interest is "grasped." It is only then, if at all, that we begin a process of criticism and selection.

Intentional action, then, emerges out of a process that is not itself conducted intentionally on every level. My past experience, for example, is continuously at work focusing my present orientation to my field of interaction. As I gain experience as an agent I build up characteristic patterns of alertness to the possibilities for action that my world holds out. These patterns of focused attention include not only explicit interests and adopted policies, but also inarticulate aversions and unnamed proclivities that trail off into whatever "subconscious" tendencies may be at work in my behavior. My past experience as an agent, that is, shapes the orientation of my present activity in a variety of ways that display a range of critical self-consciousness.

At the same time, however, my intentional action represents a selective emphasis of elements appearing in my past as an agent. Just as intentional action can be described as taking shape under the influence of my past, my past can be said to take shape in my ongoing activity as an agent; as I recognize and evaluate possibilities for action in light of my past experience, I also assess, reshape, and reappropriate that past in light of my present situation. Present actions may call in question past policies, require a break with my settled self-interpretation, and call up new networks of memory associations for me to mull over. I continually come to terms with my past in novel ways as I give shape to my present action.

Our intentional actions, then, are formed within a complex motivational background and bring that background into view, giving it focus and concreteness. An agent's life unfolds in a continuous integration of his retained past with his present experience as he explores possibilities for action presented by his immediate environment. Continuities in the content and character of action can appear across stretches of an agent's life because there is at work in each of his actions a common (though variously emphasized) background of past actions, formed policies, established interests, emotional rhythms, bodily needs, and so on. Each action is formed against this background, incorporates it in a distinctive way, and becomes part of that background as the agent's activity flows into new projects. In this way an agent's intentions always bear a reference to his past and are drawn into place in his historical identity as an agent. The complex continuities of a personal identity reflect this formation of each new action within the network of the person's past action and experience.

CONCLUSION

It has been the task of this chapter to sketch out a general picture of the psychophysical agent. In doing so we have looked at the bodily basis of the agent's activity, and noted that bodily life provides stable patterns of activity upon which intentional action is dependent and to which it remains tied. At its foundation, the bodily agent's existence assumes a pattern that is simply given for him, perpetuating itself automatically. But this stable pattern of bodily activity provides the foundation for the life of an *agent* because it permits a margin of intentional variation. In intentional action the activity that constitutes the agent's life becomes self-patterning—that is, an agent can (within the limits established by bodily life) prescribe what pattern his activity will take, and so is not only an ordered biological process but also an unfolding personal identity. An agent's life takes on its distinctive content as he operates at the nexus of his background and present field of action, working out his purposes in projects that display complex lines of thematic continuity.

But where in all this, one might ask, is the agent? In referring to an agent we are not referring simply *to* a set of actions. We attribute both intentional action and personal identity to an agent; the agent gives rise to the interwoven strands of action that we point to when we talk about his personal identity. Has our account identified the agent with his acts in such a way that we lose sight of him as their subject and source? Robert King, in developing an "intention-action model" for the concept of God, is troubled by the implications of action language at precisely this point:

> Perhaps the most notable shortcoming of the intention-action model is its tendency to absorb the person into his action, so that it is difficult to speak of the person as the subject of his action. . . . To the extent that the person intends more than one thing or has an identity which persists beyond a particular action, this approach fails us. It does not permit us to distinguish the person from his action—if only for the purpose of identifying him as the subject of his action.[10]

The key question here concerns the sense or senses in which we ought to say that the agent is the subject of his actions and is distinguishable from them. That question, of course, opens up a set of metaphysical quandaries that have occupied a great many philosophical minds. We cannot venture very far into these matters here, but we can ask (1) whether there is some reasonably clear sense in which a person should be distinguished from his actions, and (2) whether the account I have given of the human agent can do justice to this feature of our person concepts.

It seems correct to say that a person's actions disclose but do not exhaust his identity. While he expresses himself in the particular actions he undertakes, he is more than an accumulation of actions. He gives rise to his actions; they are his, but they are not him. For, first, we ascribe a wide range of actions to the agent as their "owner," and in doing so we suppose that we are dealing with a single individual, a persisting subject of reference. Second, in many instances we are ready to say that an agent could act otherwise than he does. Third, the full set of perceptions, emotions, attitudes, memories, interests, and so forth that figure in an agent's life are only imperfectly expressed in any single action.

These are important claims. A great deal remains to be said about the first two in particular, and considerable controversy surrounds proposals that interpret and develop them. The point of immediate importance, however, is that these claims pose no *special* problem for the account of the human agent offered in this chapter. Several clarifying remarks may be helpful here.

First, on the account I have given, the agent is not merely a string of intentional actions; he is a whole complex of activity both bodily and mental, autonomic and intentional. The continuities that appear among his intentional actions are rooted in continuities of bodily life, established habits, enduring interests, powerful memories, and so on. All this constitutes the dynamic structure that is the agent's life.

Second, if the agent is never solely his actions, neither is he an entity distinct from them. He bears his distinctive personal identity in and through his actions as they arise out of and focus the rest of the rest of the processes at work in his life. The agent is the whole web of these interconnected processes. If in saying this we lose the agent, then some explanation is needed of what is being lost and why we need to retain it.

Third, it might be suggested that what we lose in this case is a sense for the agent as a single individual who persists through time. I have not offered a detailed analysis of agent identity-through-time. But I have indicated the fundamental strategy and structure of such an account. As I have described the agent, his identity-through-time will be a function of complex lines of inheritance and dependence that uniquely tie him at every moment to his own past activity across its whole range (i.e., from bodily automatism to intentional action).

It is not obvious that the "enduring subject" to whom we ascribe actions must be understood as an unchanging entity rather than as a tightly woven continuity of activity. We should not quietly assume that an ongoing process must have an unchanging substratum if it is to be identified as the *same* process at different times.

Fourth, since the ghost of David Hume always haunts discussions of the self, I want to state clearly that in denying the usefulness of the notion of an underlying, residual subject I am *not* embracing a Humean skepticism about the self. Nothing in the account I have given of the human agent denies that there are real connections among the many distinguishable events that constitute the life of a self. The self is not merely a series of events that are collected in a set and given a personal name. These events are bound together both "vertically" (from automatism to intentional action) and "horizontally" (through time) by a variety of real relations—causal relations, the relation of sub-acts within an instrumental action series, the relation of intentional action to its complex motivational background, and so on. There are a number of long-standing philosophical puzzles surrounding these relations, and a fair proportion of the philosophical tradition has been devoted to analyzing them. But it is here—in considering the self as an ongoing process displaying a complex identity-through-time—that we may puzzle fruitfully over the self. Again, we must not simply assume that the only options open to us in understanding the self are a Humean bundle theory on the one hand and the notion of an underlying self-identical substance on the other.

On the account I have been developing, then, the agent is the unfolding activities of bodily life and intentional action integrated in an operative unity that we identify as the life of a distinctive individual; that is to say, the agent is nothing other than the complex system of activity that, in its extension through time, displays the intelligible patterns of bodily life and enacted personal identity. The agent is both the continuous rhythmic functioning of bodily life and the successive enactment of particular intentions; or, more precisely, he is the ongoing process that is defined by these distinguishable but integrated orders of operation. At each moment of his operation the agent is an integrated unit vertically across the scale of his activity from bodily automatism to self-conscious intentional action. And the ongoing life of the agent displays complex continuities horizontally through successive phases of his activity across this whole scale of processes (both intentional and subintentional). The agent cannot be located outside or behind this complexly layered and interconnected unity of bodily automatism and intentional action. The agent is this operative unity as it works out the pattern of its activity from one moment to the next.[11]

CHAPTER 6

God and Cosmic Organism

1. GOD AND EMBODIMENT

When theological imagination seeks to represent God as an agent of intentional actions, it must inevitably draw its materials from our understanding of persons. We can conceive of an agency that we do not exercise only by extrapolating from that agency which we claim as our own. The principle of thought at work here is hardly unique to theology: we generally seek to understand the unfamiliar in terms of the familiar.

The task of the following two chapters is to examine whether and how the account of persons that I have sketched out might be put to work in thinking about God as an agent. Virtually every theological proposal will dramatically distinguish the divine agent from human agents. In speaking of God, therefore, we inevitably modify the typical patterns of our talk about persons, selectively emphasizing and recombining characteristics of human agency so as to form the concept of an agency very unlike our own. This procedure forces upon us the question of whether our talk of God represents a possible development of the concept of an agent or instead involves so radical an alteration of the structure of that concept that it breaks down altogether.

We do not (and perhaps cannot) have at hand an adequate set of necessary conditions for any use of the concept "agent." What we do have is an account of that agency with which we are most familiar: our own. There is no reason at this point to conclude that this instance of agency is the only conceivable one. Our discussion thus far has located only the most general necessary conditions for speaking of an agent—namely, an agent must be able to act (that is, to regulate intentionally at least some aspects of his activity), and he must be a uniquely identifiable subject of speech.

Clearly some extrapolation beyond the typical characteristics of human agents is thinkable for us. As we have noted, we sometimes chafe at the limited scope of our action; the concomitant of this consciousness of limitation is the capacity to envision expanded and restructured forms of agency. The theologian can plausibly argue that human aspiration inevitably generates the idea of an agent whose scope of action is subject to no limitation that is not either necessary or self-imposed.[1] But quite apart from the ponderous business of theology, the human imagination reconstitutes our agency in unusual forms to suit its fancy. The creatures that populate fables and fairy tales often display characteristics and exercise powers of action that are simply altered forms of our own powers, modified and set in odd combinations. It is common knowledge, for example, that trolls are terribly ugly, enormously long-lived, and uniformly ill-disposed toward human beings. But beyond this, they also possess various unusual powers: some can temporarily change their shape, others can transform natural objects into beasts and monsters, and almost all use magical charms to protect themselves and their treasures. An act of kindness received from a human being, however, strips a troll of his terrible powers, at least over the individual to whom he is indebted. All this is strange, of course, but apparently conceivable as the description of a form of agency. It would be another matter if trolls were said to be bodily agents who are in several places at once or who, like Merlin, live backwards in time. Not every modification of the characteristics typical of the agency we ourselves exercise will result in a logically possible concept of an agent.

The task at hand, then, is twofold: we must consider how our account of the human agent as a psychophysical unit might be put to work in thinking about God as an agent, and we must consider whether the theistic modifications of the way we think about persons as agents leave us with a coherent concept of the divine agent.

There are, of course, a number of different ways in which a theologian might draw upon the account I have given of the psychophysical agent. I will not try to exhaust the possibilities, nor will I examine in detail each of the options I introduce; instead, I will try to map out several of the most prominent theistic possibilities and suggest some of the difficulties each will face. We can take our bearings in this process from an issue, or set of related issues, that have already commanded a good deal of attention in our discussion to this point, namely, the question of whether we can make sense of the idea of a nonbodily agent. If our understanding of human agents provides materials for our conception of the divine agent and if human agents are understood as psychophysical units, then any theistic proposal will have to sort out the senses in which it affirms and denies that the divine agent is a bodily agent. We can, therefore, set up a limited array of theistic options that represent distinct strategies of response to this issue.

In light of the discussion in Chapter 5, it is now apparent that the concept of bodiliness is not as simple as it might first appear. I have suggested that the human body is a pattern of organic activity that the human agent does not choose or intentionally enact but that permits a limited range of intentional variation in basic actions. Any agent must necessarily be an operative unit capable of intentionally modifying its own activity. In saying that we are *bodily* agents there are at least two special features of our lives to which we call attention. First, our bodiliness appears as a characteristic pattern of activity: the pattern of a living organism (we can leave it to biologists to formulate detailed rules for what should and should not count as a pattern of organic life). Second, our bodiliness appears in the givenness, the immunity to direct intentional modification, of the pattern of activity that lies at the foundation of our lives; we are bodily agents by virtue of the fact that our capacity for intentional action is rooted in a basic pattern of life that is beyond the reach of our immediate intentional control.[2]

These two aspects of our bodiliness are not identical. In our actual existence as agents, of course, they coincide and are inseparable—the given pattern of activity at the foundation of our lives is, after all, a pattern of organic activity—but bodiliness as a typical pattern of activity (i.e., organic life) must be distinguished from bodiliness as the givenness of that pattern (i.e., the inaccessibility of much of our organic life to direct intentional variation in any basic action). It is possible to suggest that an agent might be bodily in one of these respects, but not be bodily in the other—that is, one might suggest that an agent's life is founded in a given pattern of activity that establishes and limits his capacities for intentional action, and yet deny that this given pattern is a pattern of organic life. Or one might suggest that the basic pattern of an agent's life takes an organismic form, and yet insist that this basic pattern is itself intentionally enacted by the agent.

This opens up a range of four possible proposals for the theologian in responding to questions about the embodiment of God. The theologian may affirm the embodiment of God in both respects, he may deny the embodiment of God in both respects, or he may offer a mixed proposal that affirms embodiment of God in one respect and denies it in the other. It remains to be seen whether any one of these options can be successfully formulated and defended.[3]

2. GOD AS COSMIC ORGANISM

It is prudent initially to see how far a theologian might go in granting the bodiliness of God. Can we map out a proposal that defuses the embodiment challenge altogether by simply granting that God is embodied in both the respects I have distinguished? This would be to argue that God can be understood not simply as a personal agent but as a *person* (i.e., as a psychophysical agent). Justice must be done, however, to the character of God as the *divine* person. The difficult task set for such a proposal is to modify the pattern of agency that we are familiar with in human persons so as to generate a "theologically adequate" concept of God, but to stop short of modifying this pattern so radically as to no longer speak of a psychophysical agent at all.[4]

This may seem an impossible task, and from some theological perspectives the whole proposal can only appear to be an impossibly flimsy compromise, but it will be helpful to consider briefly how one might propose to carry through this project. It is not uncommon for theologians to call upon the relation of an agent to his body as a model for the relation of God to the world.[5] One might, that is, suggest that the world be thought of as "God's body." This analogy could be developed in a dualistic way: one might treat God and world as inherently different entities that happen to be so closely associated as to form a single life. But the proposal that God be thought of as embodied in the universe is not necessarily tied to mind-body dualism. One might argue instead that God and world constitute a complex psychophysical unity.[6] This, however, will produce a considerably more radical revision of traditional theism than would a dualistic development of the same suggestion.

Suppose, then, that we think of God and world as a single, indissolubly unified, though unimaginably complex psychophysical agent. What will be required if we are to develop this view? The first point to note is that we must draw as close a parallel as possible between the universe (all that is) and a living organism. It will not do to portray the universe simply as an aggregate of many individuals that may interact with each other but that do not combine in any overall harmonious function. Rather we must see the universe as an organic whole the many constituents of which are integrated in a single operative unity. This will be a point of particular vulnerability for this theological proposal. Clearly, the project of conceiving of God as a psychophysical agent will be threatened if this picture of the totality of things is seriously called in question.[7] It would be very difficult, however, to say how far one might back away from these claims about the organic unity of the universe and still have a viable basis for talk of God and world as a psychophysical unity. That is a debate I will not try to conduct here.

If we can successfully construe our world as a single, functionally unified individual, then we may speak of God as the agent whose life is grounded in and constituted by the cosmic organism. Given a non-dualist understanding of the bodily agent as a psychophysical unit, God cannot be said to exist as a distinct being apart from and over against the world. Just as the human agent is not to be identified with an immaterial substance that controls the body, so God is not to be thought of as a supernatural power who intervenes "from above" to act upon the physical world. If we refuse to picture the human agent as a "ghost in the machine," then we should no longer represent God as a "ghost in the universe."[8] To say that the world is God's body is to say that the processes unfolding in the universe are the processes of God's life, that God does not exist except in and through these processes.

On the other hand, God will not be identified with the physical universe in any sense that precludes his being the bearer of a distinctive personal identity as an agent. It will not be enough to say simply that God *is* the organically unified system of activity that constitutes the totality of things, for as I have already argued, an organic system of activity (i.e, a body) is not an agent unless it operates intentionally in at least a small range of its activities. As the agent whose life is the world process, God is not to be located outside that process; his actions are events within the universe, and not events that break in upon the universe. But God's actions are not merely the occurrence of certain processes in the physical universe; rather, they are the *enactment* of those processes for the achievement of his purposes. Just as human agents possess a capacity to intentionally vary certain of the processes that constitute bodily life, so God can intentionally regulate at least some of the processes that constitute the universe as an organic totality.

God is, in this sense, creative. His activity as agent organizes the various processes at work in the universe into patterns expressive of his purpose for the overall achievement of the "world process." His capacity for intentional action may extend far down into the stable patterns that lie at the foundation of his activity as well. If so, his capacity to realize his intentions for the "life" of the universe (which is his life) will be vastly greater than the power we exercise over the formation of our lives. The divine agent, that is, will be profoundly self-creative. In addition, the divine agent may be eminently self-conscious. His awareness of the individual constituents that are functionally interrelated in the cosmic organism will be vastly more detailed and sympathetic than any human self-knowledge or interpersonal understanding.[9] Given this concern for the constituents that are united in his life, God's intentional activity will be eminently well-considered, maximizing the realization of preferred possibilities in any situation and minimizing the sacrifice of positive values. God will be continuously at work throughout the whole range of his intentional capacities, bringing into actuality all of the highest possibilities contained in any moment of world process.

But while God is an eminently creative agent, he cannot be said to be the creator of the universe in any traditional theological sense. God may shape, direct, and organize the world process to a degree that far exceeds the limited self-creativity we exercise in our own lives, but he does not bring the universe into being or sustain it in its existence (though he may preserve certain of the patterns of cosmic process that he purposefully enacts). Since the "life" of the cosmos is the life of God, God cannot be said to bring the cosmos into being without implying that he brings himself into being. Not even the boldest enthusiast for paradox, however, is likely to embrace the claim that God creates himself *ex nihilo*.

Furthermore, if God is to be bodily in both of the respects in which human beings are bodily, then his creative activity must finally be rooted in a pattern of life immune to intentional variation. God's powers of action may be of vastly greater scope and significance than ours, but they will nonetheless be finite. Though God is eminently self-creative, he is not unconditionally so. God's creative will is limited to possibilities established by the subintentional processes in which his life is grounded. In this respect, God's creativity is directly parallel to our own. The divine agent works with what is given for him, and must do the best he can with it. God does not freely commit himself to an intimate and vulnerable association with the world's process: he *is* that process. God's life is not complete apart from the life of the world, any more than the human agent's life is complete apart from bodily life. In the full expression of the positive possibilities of the world process lies the fulfillment of God's own existence. The unfolding world process will be the process of God's own self-realization.

There is a great deal more that might be said in developing this account of God as a psychophysical agent, but enough has been said here to indicate the key structures of this type of proposal. We need to note briefly some of its vulnerabilities. There are, of course, difficulties with the central analogies upon which the proposal trades. I pointed out initially that one may question whether "the totality of things" can plausibly be construed as a functionally unified organism. There is a complementary problem that must also be mentioned. If the universe is construed as a cosmic organism, it appears that its unity will be too close to allow for the integrity of creatures as independent centers of activity interacting with God—that is, not only does our world appear to be too loose an association of individuals to pass as a cosmic organism, but a living body appears to require too tight a unity to permit the emergence of its constituents as agents in their own right. If one stresses the organic unity of creatures as the body of God, one threatens their standing as distinct individuals over against God. Yet if one stresses the interpersonal character of our relation to God, then one weakens the organismic unity of the world as a single individual.

Proponents of the organismic analogy have not been blind to these tensions. Charles Hartshorne, in what remains the most powerful development of this view, explicitly takes on the task of combining mind-body and interpersonal analogies in his account of the relation of God and world. In his early work Hartshorne develops a panpsychism that treats persons (both human and divine) as complex societies of lower order centers of activity.[10] His case is strengthened by the evident correctness of the suggestion that a human life is a complex organization of many subordinate units of activity which are organized hierarchically in the overall structure of bodily life. If these subcenters of activity are to be agents, however, each must be allowed a unity of operation and a distinctness of intention that is sufficient to mark it out as a unique individual. Yet these unique individuals must also be so intimately interconnected that, as a whole, they constitute an irreducibly unified life. This "super-individual" is not an additional entity conjoined to the many "sub-individuals" (i.e., subordinate individuals) who are its constituents; rather, it *is* these many sub-individuals in their interrelatedness. The functional unit as a whole possesses a unique identity as a subject of experience and agent of intentional actions.

Puzzles abound at this point. Can a single event be an action in precisely the same sense for both the sub-individuals and the super-individual? If so, can they be distinct agents?[11] Are the actions of sub-individuals to be understood as enactments of the super-individual's intentions? If so, are the sub-individuals agents in their own right at all? Is the action of the super-individual simply the accumulated effect of the actions of many sub-individuals? If so, is the super-individual an agent in any significant sense? Does the super-individual act by somehow influencing the actions of the many sub-individuals? If so, is the super-individual surreptitiously being treated as a distinct entity that acts upon the society of many sub-individuals? The effect of such questions is to apply pressure to each side of the social-individual hybrid that Hartshorne has produced. Despite the imaginative skill of Hartshorne's discussion, the central tension remains. It is not clear that a society of distinct agents can be so closely bound together as to take on the unity of a single organism. Nor is it clear that the constituents of a living organism can possess an independence of action sufficient to constitute a society of selves.

The magnitude of this problem for the theology of organism could be determined only by a careful and extended study. The notion of a living organism would have to be clarified, for example, before we could reliably say how far one can carry the thought experiment of treating an individual organism as a society of distinct agents. It is certainly the case that theological reflection often combines analogies in unusual ways with the intention of approximating a reality that we cannot readily grasp.[12] Austin Farrer offers a caveat that is to the point here: "The vice of metaphysical argument is to reject your opponent's positions because they involve the stretching of natural terms, while overlooking or disguising the equally stretched senses implicit in your own."[13] It is important to remember that metaphysical argument is an ongoing experiment with the elastic properties of language. Nonetheless, there is some reason to wonder whether, once the necessary qualifications have been made, the divine agent any longer resembles a psychophysical unit. The first of the two respects in which we set out to claim embodiment for God (as a living organism) may be subtly and progressively abandoned in the face of the demands of experiential and theological adequacy.

If these problems with the organismic analogy could be resolved, there would nonetheless remain certain obvious and important theological objections to the proposal that God be thought of as a bodily agent. Remember that our project here is to conceive of God as a bodily agent in *both* of the senses we originally identified. This requires that God's life be rooted in a basic pattern of activity that he does not choose or intentionally enact, but that establishes and limits his capacity for intentional action;[14] this quite clearly presents us with a distinctly finite God. The appeal of this might lie in the image of a deity closely associated with the creature, open to the creature's influence, and sympathetically identified with the creature's destiny—a God whose life cannot be disassociated from the creature's life, and whose realization of his highest possibilities is necessarily linked to the fulfillment of the creature in the harmony of a single achievement. This stands in sharp contrast to the remote perfection of the God of scholastic theism, a deity (it might be suggested) who is walled up in the private enjoyment of an impenetrable self-sufficiency.

Let it be granted that language which places God in mutually affecting relations with creatures is prominent in Jewish and Christian devotion. We might also grant that high Medieval theism, preoccupied with a concept of metaphysical perfection constructed out of Aristotle (and, less self-consciously, out of Plotinus), found it difficult to accommodate these features of the Christian religious tradition. But it is not obvious that the only way of doing justice to the God who is compassionately involved with creatures is to identify God's life with the totality of finite things. Scholastic theism has been charged with failing to speak of the God of Christian faith because it failed to do justice to God's "humanity." The suggestion that God is a finite but preeminent psychophysical agent might be charged with the complementary error of failing to do justice to God's deity, for on this account, God may be a peculiarly inclusive and powerful person, but he is nonetheless confronted with the same kind of limitations we are. His agency is rooted in subintentional patterns of activity that he does not choose or intentionally enact. The question "Why does God's active existence take the form it does?" can only in part be answered by pointing to God's intentions. As with human agents, we finally confront a brute givenness at the foundation of God's existence.

One may simply rest with this inexplicability of the cosmic agent. One can refuse to offer any answer to the question "Why does God's life and, *ex hypothesi*, the universe display this basic pattern and operate within this limited range of possibilities rather than some other?" A question of this general type, of course, powers each of the various forms of cosmological argument. Cosmological arguments establish lines of explanatory regress back to a being who is self-explanatory in whatever respect is required by the particular form of regress involved (e.g., in terms of motion, efficient causation, contingent existence, etc.). The defects of this bit of natural theology are well known; not the least of them is the vulnerability of such arguments to a simple refusal to offer an explanation that claims absolute finality and completeness. That, in effect, is what the proponent of a finite deity must do. But this is an awkward posture for him to assume, given his willingness to speak of the world as a single all-inclusive entity. About this entity, which is no mere thing but rather the divine agent, the "cosmological question"—"Why this pattern of existence, given that other possibilities are conceivable?"—can surely arise, just as it can about human agents. The characteristic theological point is *not* that the question "Why?", when asked about the pattern of God's existence, simply has no answer; rather, it is that in principle no answer to the cosmological question can be sought outside God himself. One may not be impressed by efforts to produce a coercive chain of inference from finite beings to a divine ground of their existence, but one may nevertheless insist that part of what one *means* by "God" (whether or not one can "prove" that there is a God) is a being (1) in whom an ultimate explanation of the existence and nature of all other beings can be found, and (2) whose existence and nature require no explanation by appeal to any other being or beings. God is in this sense the originative ground of existence beyond which it will be impossible to go in seeking explanation for why there are the sorts of beings there are or why there are any finite beings at all. If, however, God is understood as a psychophysical agent who is bodily in both of the respects in which human agents are bodily, then this clearly cannot be said of him. God becomes, in the most important respects, a being of the same kind as we—a finite person.

3. GOD AS SELF-EMBODYING

It is a matter for argument whether the concept of God as a finite person can do justice to the principal concerns at work in the devotional traditions of Christianity. I will not try to develop those issues here. There is, in any case, an apparent remedy for some of the difficulties we have discussed. We can deny that God's intentional activity is subject to any limitation that is not self-imposed. This would be to deny that there is any given, subintentional pattern of activity that establishes and limits the range of God's actions; rather, in God's life the capacity for intentional action runs right to the "bottom" of his activity: even the most stable patterns of God's activity are intentionally enacted and purposefully maintained. Moreover, we will want to say not only that all of God's activity is intentional, but also that all of God's intentional actions are free in every relevant sense.[15] God, then, is understood as an agent of unrestricted self-creativity, an agent whose pattern of activity is at no point inaccessible to intentional regulation but rather is in every respect freely self-prescribed.

Having said this, a theologian may still suggest that God and world be thought of as constituting a complex psychophysical unit, although he will have changed the terms of this proposal in a decisive way. The world no longer provides at any level of its ongoing activity structures that are simply given for God. We now say instead that God intentionally enacts the pattern of the world's activity as the basic structure of his own life. Whatever limitations upon God's possibilities may be involved in this pattern of existence are the result of God's own intentional self-limitation. God freely chooses to give his life the structure of a complex organism, uniting various subcenters of activity in a single functionally integrated whole. Just as before, God will not exist as a complete being outside the life of the world. We will now be able to say, however, that God could exist without the world, for God could constitute his life differently, giving it some other fundamental pattern that did not take the form of a social organism. But given that God has constituted his life in this way, he is who he is by virtue of choosing to exist as the cosmic organism, the agent whose life is the world.

We now have a mixed response to our question about divine embodiment. Embodiment is being denied of God in the second of the two respects I initially distinguished and affirmed of God in the first—that is, embodiment is denied of God if embodiment means limitation by a given, subintentional pattern of activity, whereas embodiment is affirmed of God if embodiment means that God's life takes the form of a unified organic process. God is an absolutely self-determining agent who continuously enacts his own bodily life.

We will take a closer look at the idea of an absolutely self-determining agent in a moment. First it will be useful to offer a few remarks on this modified theology of organism. In this form, the proposal that the world be thought of as God's body does avoid the difficulties associated with treating God as an inherently limited psychophysical agent. Given this more qualified account of God's embodiment, the only answer that can be offered to the question of why God's active existence assumes the pattern it does is that God so intends it. The fundamental pattern of the divine life is to be attributed to God's own free self-determination—a self-determination that may involve intentional self-limitation. There can be in principle no move behind or beyond God's sovereign will in seeking to understand why God's life (and, *ex hypothesi,* the world) displays just this fundamental structure.

However, once we have denied that the world at any level constitutes a pattern of activity beyond the reach of God's intentions, we may well wonder why we should speak of God as embodied at all. Having given up the attempt to argue for divine embodiment in the second sense, is there any point continuing to claim it in the first?

We have already seen that the organismic model must be significantly qualified by a concern to preserve an independence of action for the creaturely constituents of God's life. The world may be God's body, but that body must be of such a sort that it can unite in a single operative unit constituents that are themselves centers of intentional action. Once this has been said, we may wonder whether the concept of organism has been so thoroughly modified as to leave little distinction between this theology of divine embodiment and a more traditional theism. On the one hand, we say "God enacts the world as his body," but we add the proviso that this body must be understood as (at least in part) a society of creaturely agents in and through which the divine agent lives his life; on the other hand, we might say "God creates a world that includes finite agents whose existence he sustains and whose lives he subtly shapes and guides." In either case God establishes and sustains the creature's existence and, in particular, establishes and sustains finite agents as centers of activity with a limited independence of operation; in either case God concerns himself with the creature's destiny and works out his purposes through the creature's life; and in either case the scope of God's action is universal. God's sympathetic intention embraces every creature, appreciating its particular interests and seeking its fulfillment within the overarching pattern of the divine purposes in creation.

The key difference in these doctrines lies in the extent to which God's life is identified with that of the world. The distinctive content of the image of the world as God's body seems to lie in the insistence that God's activity and interest is exhausted in his involvement with creatures. God's active existence is totally identified with the world as he guides its development toward a harmonious achievement. The theological motive for urging this way of linking God and world might, as we noted, be a concern to take seriously God's openness to his creatures.[16] This proposal does provide an imaginative context in which talk of divine love—and even divine suffering and vulnerability—can be supported conceptually. But it is not necessary to identify God's life exclusively with his activity in and through the creature in order to do justice to the depth and intimacy of God's relation to the world. It is not obvious that God must live through the creature in order to enter sympathetically into the life of the creature. On the contrary, one might argue that God establishes a relationship with creatures not out of a need to complete his own life, but out of a love that expresses the character of the completeness he enjoys. That God's life can be complete even without creatures does not entail either that he must exist without them or that if he chooses to create finite persons he is barred from relations with them that affect his own life. On the other hand, if God's active existence is exhaustively identified with a world process that bears his life, then the possibility of speaking of the divine agent at all is dependent upon the viability of the organismic analogy, since God's life is given no content apart from the life of the world through which he operates as a bodily agent. If the world cannot be convincingly portrayed as a functionally unified individual, then the divine agent disappears along with the cosmic organism.

The vulnerabilities of this mixed proposal about divine embodiment might be forced upon us if it could be shown that an agent must (logically) be embodied in the first of the two respects initially distinguished; that is, if one of the necessary conditions for forming any concept of an agent were that the basic pattern of the agent's life take a form that we would recognize as organic life, then the theist might well decide simply to do the best he can with the analogy of cosmic organism. But given our discussions to this point, it is difficult to know how one might make a convincing case for the claim that organic life is a necessary condition for agency. Perhaps it could be argued that the concept of an intentional action is the concept of an intentional bodily movement and therefore of a modification of organic processes. This would be to argue for a *logical* rule of the form "no bodily movement, no intentional action." But this rule does not apply even in our own case: many of our actions are not bodily movements. We conduct an endless variety of projects for thought that neither require nor become full-fledged bodily actions. It must be acknowledged that projects for thought are often undertaken for the sake of bodily action, and that our lives of unshared reflection and unenacted plans remain rooted in a wider context of vital interests as bodily agents, but it nevertheless remains true that we ourselves continually undertake actions that are not overt bodily movements.

It might be argued that even intentional *mental* activities are, at some level, always bodily actions as well. A neurophysiologist might explain that conscious activity is correlated in certain regular ways with organic events. To speak of intentional activity that is not rooted in physical activity is to sever a link that as a matter of fact we always find in our experience. But while our "mental actions" do apparently involve complex organic processes, purposive mental activity is not a subspecies of intentional bodily action. I do intend a bodily event in intentionally raising my arm, but I do not intend any bodily event in working out a bit of mental arithmetic, even though this no doubt involves the stimulation of nerve complexes in the brain. Perhaps we could be persuaded by an "identity theorist" to say that in referring to a mental act we are referring to an event in the brain, but it will not follow that in speaking of a mental act the meaning of what we say is equivalent to the meaning of statements about brain events. Nor is it clear that every statement about intentional mental activity (e.g., imagining a tropical paradise; remembering scenes from childhood) *entails* statements about physical events (whether overt bodily movements or minute physiological processes).

The key point to keep in mind is that in asking whether we can speak of intentional activity that is not bodily activity we are looking for logical connections between concepts, not merely for observed connections between events in our experience. We have already considered arguments to the effect that references to intentional actions are logically tied to references to bodies. In particular we considered the claim that we can only identify a subject of intentional actions by identifying a material body. But we saw that the demand for identification could be met by a nonbodily agent in a number of ways as well. It appears logically possible, then, to speak of actions that involve no processes that we would recognize as the organic life of a bodily agent.

If it is reasonable to suppose that an agent's life might be rooted in a basic pattern of activity different in kind from our own, it must be acknowledged immediately that we will not be able to say very much about such an agent. Though our activity is not exhausted by bodily life and takes forms that cannot be reduced to bodily processes, nonetheless we have no ready model for the basic pattern of activity of a nonbodily agent. The life pattern of such an agent must remain obscure to us. There is no reason, however, why we cannot speak of such an agent as long as the formal structure of the concepts of agency and intention is preserved. We can form the concept of an agent as long as we can speak of an integrated unit of activity that is capable of intentionally regulating at least some stretches of its own operation. We can refer to this agent as long as we can provide a context in which the agent can be uniquely identified. And we can give a concrete content to the life of this agent as long as we can ascribe intentional actions to him that allow us to characterize his distinctive identity as an agent. All this may be possible even if we can say very little about the basic pattern of activity at the foundation of the agent's life or about how his activity brings about its intended results. The concept of a nonbodily agent may be coherent and even quite rich in spite of the fact that it will inevitably be incomplete.

CHAPTER 7

God and the Perfection of Agency

1. THE PERFECTION OF AGENCY

There appears to be no compelling reason to think of God as a self-embodying cosmic organism. If we deny that God's life is rooted in a pattern of activity beyond the reach of his intentional control, then little is gained by affirming that God gives his life the form of a complex organism. This leaves us with a third position which stands as the polar opposite of that with which we began. We first considered the suggestion that God be thought of as a psychophysical unit, embodied in both of the key respects in which persons are embodied. Now we turn to a theism that denies that God is embodied in either of these respects, that holds God to be an agent whose basic pattern of activity neither takes the form of organic life nor is at any point beyond the reach of his intentional regulation.

It is important to note that when we deny embodiment of God in the crucial second sense, we affirm the perfection of his capacity to enact his life intentionally. In order to be an agent at all, any individual must be able to order segments of his own activity purposefully (i.e., be able to act). If God's life is not rooted in a given bodily structure, then all of his activity will be intentional action. In this way, one of the defining properties of agency is radicalized and completed in the divine agent. This suggests that there might be other possibilities inherent in the concept of an agent that are fully realized in God. My purpose in this chapter, therefore, is not simply to develop an account of God as a nonbodily agent, but to explore how we might conceive of God as that individual in whose life agency is brought to perfection.

This is a familiar pattern of theological argument. If we can establish an ascending scale of perfection, and if it makes sense to assert that this scale has a maximum, then we can identify God with ultimate perfection so defined. Throughout its history, the theological tradition has worked out variations upon this fundamental program for theistic reflection. Most often the scale of perfection to which theologians have appealed has been a scale of being. Thomas Aquinas, for example, constructed a metaphysical scheme in which all beings can be ranked in the degree to which the act of existing (*esse*) is expressed within the network of properties that define what kind of thing that being is (its nature, or essence—*essentia*). To be living rather than inanimate, or to be a rational life rather than a merely animal life, is *to be* to a greater degree. Given such a scheme, one can identify God as the essential expression of existence. God is not *a* being, God simply *is* Being—that is, God is self-subsistent Being-itself (*ipsum esse per se subsistens*).[1]

In the discussion that follows, I will appeal to a scale of agency rather than to a scale of being. One advantage of this approach is that it avoids the problematic metaphysical machinery at work in talk of degrees of existence. A scale of agency requires only that there are properties of agents that (a) can be displayed in varying degrees, (b) represent enhancements of an individual's agency when displayed to a greater degree, and (c) increase toward an intrinsic maximum beyond which it is impossible to go in further enhancing the mode or power of one's agency. There is nothing comparable here to the reification of Being as a reality distinct from its particular instances; rather, in speaking of the perfection of agency we mean simply "that agent in whom these agent-properties reach their maximal expression."[2]

There are three properties of agents that I will discuss in exploring the concept of the divine agent. First, I will develop somewhat more fully the idea of an agent whose capacity to regulate his own activity is not limited by any given pattern of life. Because this agent's activity will be unrestrictedly intentional, we may speak of him as "radically self-creative." Second, an agent's ability to structure his life will also be enhanced by an increase in the degree to which he can introduce meaningful order into his activity. Agency is expanded not only by increasing the depth of an agent's self-regulation, but also by increasing the degree to which he can enact his life as a unified whole. This opens up the possibility of thinking of God as an agent whose life is maximally unified and harmonious. Third, agency is enhanced by increasing the range of actions that an agent is capable of performing. The power to act reaches its maximum in an agent who has open to him the widest possible scope of action. As the perfection of agency, then, God will be radically self-creative (he intends all that he is), fully unified as a self (the whole of his life displays the harmony of a single intention), and all-powerful (his activity faces no limitation that is not either necessary or self-imposed).

2. THE SELF-CREATIVITY OF GOD

At this point we need to explore more systematically the idea of an agent whose intentional activity is not dependent upon and limited by any subintentional vital pattern. As I noted in discussing the mixed embodiment proposal in Chapter 6, God's capacity to regulate the pattern of his activity extends down to the very foundation of his life. At no point does intentional action disappear into the automatism of a life pattern that is given for him and binding upon his projects. Even the most dependable structures that appear in his activity are structures of intentional action. The divine agent exercises an unrestricted freedom to enact his life as his project. This must mean, as I indicated earlier, that God both intends all that he is and freely commits himself to all that he intends (in every relevant sense of the term "free"). God, therefore, is a radically self-creative agent.

Some caution is required in speaking of God as "self-creative," however, for this phrase is potentially misleading. God can be said to be self-creative in the sense that he determines the content of his own existence. God, that is, freely prescribes the pattern of activity that constitutes his life. Human agents may also be said to be self-creative in this sense, though the range of our self-creativity is inevitably limited. Our finitude consists precisely in this, that our capacity to direct our activity is restricted by the very life pattern that establishes our capacity to act at all. Though the unique personal identity of a human agent expresses his capacity to prescribe the pattern of his own life, that personal identity represents an ad hoc development of given resources. By contrast, God's self-creativity is "in-finite," or unlimited, since his capacity to enact his life extends throughout the whole range of his activity without restriction by a subintentional life pattern. We are the agents of our lives to a limited degree. God is the agent of his life without restriction.

Neither God nor any other agent can be self-creative, however, if this means that the agent brings himself into being *ex nihilo*. This obviously makes no sense, since there is no agent to perform the creative act until the creative act has been performed. This suggests some further reflections. It also appears that a radically self-creative agent cannot be brought into being through the creative act of another agent, since the defining mark of a radically self-creative agent is that every moment of his life consists of free intentional action. If an agent's life has a beginning, however, then there must be some initial phase and original orientation of activity that is the foundation from which all subsequent activity develops. This initial orientation of activity cannot be self-prescribed, since until it begins there is no self (no agent) to prescribe it. But if the first phase of the agent's activity is given through the action of another, then it either will not be intentional action or will not be free. In either case the created agent will not be a radically self-creative agent. Hence, a radically self-creative agent cannot have a beginning either through his own act or through that of another.

A number of further points follow from this directly. If a radically self-creative agent exists, then he has always existed. By the same token, if no such agent exists, then none will ever exist. Note, however, that we cannot conclude from this that if such an agent exists then he will always exist. Nothing has yet been said that would rule out the possibility of self-destruction for a radically self-creative being; it appears that such an agent could enact a pattern of existence that includes an end to that existence. An additional argument is needed if we are to conclude that God, understood as the perfection of agency, will exist forever. We might argue, for example, that unending continuity of action is an essential (i.e., necessary) property of God (see sec. 4 following). In that case, existing eternally as a self-creative agent would be part of what it is to *be* God; ceasing to exist would simply not be an open option for the divine agent.

Whether or not one makes this particular claim, we can give a significant sense to the ascription of aseity to God, for even if it were possible that God might end his own life, he will not be vulnerable to having his life ended by any other agent or by any combination of circumstances that he does not control. We might claim that this is a consequence simply of God's radical self-creativity, since the continued existence of a radically self-creative agent will not be subject to the unavoidable dangers that accompany a fixed life pattern. There is no need to argue this out at length, however, for if we understand God as the perfection of agency, then we are committed to claiming that God is the omnipotent creator of all beings other than himself, and this entails that God's continued existence cannot be dependent upon the actions of any other being unless he intends that it be. Rather, God is an ontologically independent agent, and in this sense exists from himself (*a se*): his existence has no sustaining ground beyond his own continuous enactment of the pattern of his life. God is always actively realizing his intentions for his life in an ongoing self-enactment that is without beginning and, if he so wills it, without end.

It is tempting in this connection to redefine and reissue the classical claim that God is *actus purus*. We cannot, of course, say that God is *actus purus* in the scholastic sense—that is, that he is pure actuality from which all becoming is excluded. God's actuality is not a static and immutable possession, but rather a dynamic activity. God is "pure act," however, insofar as his life consists entirely of self-determining activity. And since God is ontologically independent, this freely self-determining activity is also fully self-sustaining. God's life is both thoroughly intentional and invulnerably vital. God is pure act, then, in the sense that he exists from himself, without support or ground, in autonomous self-creativity.

Having said this, we can also note senses in which God can be said to be beyond becoming, changeless, and simple. First, God is beyond becoming in the sense that he need never (unless he so chooses) pursue an end that he cannot immediately enact. Becoming, in at least one sense of the term, implies a delayed realization of the end of one's activity, there being some unavoidable intermediary process that connects the agent with the outcome he intends. God, however, does not face any given limitation upon his capacity for basic action and so does not need to employ indirect means to bring about any end that might, if he were capable, be directly enacted. As a result, God need not cast his life in the form of a progressive approach to various future goals; he may choose to undertake only those projects that can be realized in being enacted, without requiring any period of development. God is not, therefore, necessarily committed to becoming (in this limited sense), even though he has his very being in action.

It must also be allowed, however, that God can commit himself to becoming, to development, if he should so choose to structure his activity. It is at this point that the traditional doctrine of God as changeless actuality becomes *theologically* problematic. Should we say that God is *actus purus* in the scholastic sense, we would not be able to understand his relation to creatures and their history except in his functions as the Ultimate Cause, reducing potentiality to actuality in other things without himself undergoing any change. This makes it difficult to do justice, however, to the richness of the relationship between God and humankind that appears in the narrative sources and devotional traditions of Judaism and Christianity. We must not exclude the possibility that God may establish a relation to creatures in which he is genuinely affected by them and yet does not cease to be God.

Second, we can say that God is beyond change in the sense that he is capable of radical consistency in his actions. This does not mean that his life consists of an unimaginative reiteration of some ideal pattern of activity, but it does mean that in all of his actions, however varied their particular aims, he can remain faithful to his central intention. Insofar as God's purposes remain constant throughout the endless diversity of his actions, we can speak of divine immutability—understanding "immutability" to mean not frozen inactivity, but rather absolute consistency of character and complete fidelity to his intentions.

Third, we may say that God is simple insofar as all of his actions are drawn together in the unity of a single intention: he can enact his life without discordant or irreducibly divergent lines of action. The divine simplicity will consist in the overarching coherence of God's life as a single project.

On this account, both God's changelessness and simplicity are expressions of the unity of his life as an agent. Nothing has been said so far, however, that would lead us to conclude that God's life is unified in this way. A radically self-creative agent appears to be capable not only of ideal unity but also of extreme changeableness and profound self-revision. This is a problem to which I will return at length in a moment. First, however, a brief word about God and time is needed here in connection with these remarks on changelessness and simplicity.

It has often been claimed by theists that God is eternal, not simply in the sense that he exists at all times but in the stronger sense that he exists atemporally. This, of course, is not simply to assert that God does not change through time, so that his past and future always have a qualitatively identical content; rather, it is to say that God is in no way extended in time, whether as a pattern of change or as static immutability. There is no time order in God's life, no before and after, no "was" and "will be." The difficulties with this conception have been explored at length by others.[3] It is in any case very difficult to see how an understanding of eternity as timelessness can be combined with a conception of God as an agent. The concept of an action certainly appears to entail a time order. We cannot think of intentional action except as a temporally extended stretch of activity intended as a meaningful unit. Talk of an agent who has his being in his intentional activity and yet who exists atemporally appears to be a contradiction in terms. Such an agent will act, but none of his actions will be performed before or after any of the others, nor will any single action have any temporal extension whatsoever. This agent will have his existence in "timeless activity." And that appears to be on the same logical footing as saying that the content of this agent's timeless activity is an endless and delighted squaring of circles.

If we are to speak of God as an agent of intentional actions, we are committed to thinking of God's life as having a temporal order. It would be too simple, however, to say that the time order of God's life coincides with the time order we describe for our own. The concepts of time that we employ in everyday discourse, not to mention in philosophy and physics, are too complex to allow us to rest with so simple a statement. But it does seem clear that the life of an agent must display some irreversible temporal order. If to talk of the eternity of God's life is to talk of God's relation to time at all, then in ascribing eternity we can only mean that God exists at all times without beginning and without end.

An equation of temporality with imperfection is not as obvious today as it was for Neoplatonists and the Christian theology they influenced. Perhaps the passage of time is inevitably tragic for us, since it measures the unfolding of a life process that inevitably exhausts itself and ends, but it need not be so for a radically self-creative agent. God may enact a pattern of life that fills time with a content so rich that human imagination cannot conceive of it and so vital that even infinite temporal extension cannot impoverish it.[4]

3. THE UNITY OF GOD

So far we have been exploring the suggestion that God be thought of as an agent whose capacity for intentional action is not rooted in a subintentional life structure. On this account, God has an unrestricted power to enact his life intentionally, making possible the "changelessness" and "simplicity" just mentioned. But it also makes possible dramatic shifts of intention and profound reorganizations of life pattern. It appears that a radically self-creative agent might utterly transform the character of his activity at any moment.

Any agent organizes and reorganizes the pattern of his activity as he moves from action to action. A bodily agent, however, can reshape his life only within the settled context of a basic structure that is given for him. Consistencies of activity are established at a subintentional level in the life of a bodily agent, and these consistencies provide a setting for coherent action. All this changes when we speak of a radically self-creative agent, whose intentional actions will not be tied to a structure of bodily life that would enforce at least a minimal consistency upon his operation as an agent. Such an agent will be able to reorganize his activity with a peculiar thoroughness, and so will be capable of stunning revisions in the pattern of his life. Just how complete might this self-reorganization be? Might such an agent persistently modify his activity in ways that depart dramatically from his past? Here we seem to contemplate a deity with an infinitely split personality. Can this unsettling possibility be ruled out?

There are two complementary ways of responding to this problem. One is based strictly upon the necessary conditions for any use of the concept "agent." The other points to a distinctive feature of the concept of God as the perfection of agency.

The first point can be expressed most simply by noting that an agent is a unified and enduring individual. A series of discontinuous actions cannot constitute the life of an agent. When we refer to an agent we are not merely suggesting that a number of otherwise unrelated events can be gathered together and assigned membership in a set. An agent is necessarily a more integral unit than this. As we saw in Chapter 5, an agent's life is a complexly layered process that successively posits its own next phase in communication with its past and with its field of interaction. The agent exists as an integrated structure of activity that is continuous through time. There will be logical limits, therefore, upon the scope of change that can be embraced within the life of a single agent. Some minimum degree of continuity is required if a series of events is to constitute the life of an agent.

It is probably impossible to fix these logical limits with precision. Questions about personal identity through time are notoriously complex and resistant to resolution by appeal to simple criteria.[5] Nonetheless, it is clear that there are significant difficulties with the suggestion that an agent might utterly restructure his existence at any moment. The more radical this reorganization of activity becomes, the more profound the problems will be for describing this agent as an individual who endures through time. At some point, depending upon the particular features of the case, we will no longer be able to refer to *an* agent. Just what we should say in this situation will depend on the nature of the proposal that has been made. Perhaps we will say that one agent has perished and another has risen from his ashes. More likely we will say that the language of agency has broken down into incoherence, so that we cannot speak of an agent at all in this case. This might happen, for example, if we were to claim that a particular agent could utterly disregard his own past actions, so that each new phase of his activity would be initiated without reference to those that preceded it. This agent would break continuity with his past at every moment in which his activity takes a new turn. But in this case it would be impossible to give meaning to talk of a past that is *his*. The result is that we have defined a pattern of life for this agent that precludes him from being a unified individual—that is, precludes him from being an agent.

If we grant this demand for continuity of action, must we abandon the notion of a radically self-creative agent? Is that notion in fact incoherent, attributing to this agent a capacity for radical self-modification that turns out to be incompatible with his being an agent at all? We need not rush to this conclusion. In calling an agent radically self-creative we are not saying that the range of actions open to him is at every moment utterly unstructured and unfocused; rather, we are saying that his range of action is not rooted in a life pattern that he does not intentionally enact. This is perfectly compatible with the general requirement that an agent's life display a connectedness and continuity through time sufficient to constitute an enduring individual existence. In Chapter 5 it became clear that the unity of an agent is crucially dependent upon the ongoing role of his past in giving shape to his present activity. But this continuity with one's past pattern of life need not result from a subintentional perpetuation of given structures of activity (e.g., a pattern of organic life). Rather, this continuity may be grounded in the agent's appropriation of his past in his present intentional actions. Such is the case with the continuities that constitute a distinctive personal identity. The personal identity of a bodily agent, of course, is always based upon and woven around the subintentional regularities of bodily life. In the life of a radically self-creative agent, the continuity of his activity will be rooted solely in intentions that both grasp his past and structure his future. The unity of a radically self-creative agent's life, therefore, will entirely be a unity of intention and character. This agent will have personal identity, but no bodily identity.

If we grant that the life of a radically self-creative agent must be at least minimally unified and coherent, we nonetheless leave open the possibility of dramatic transformations in this agent's life pattern. A radically self-creative agent could survey his past patterns of action and set out in a new direction formed in reaction against what he had been. Though the change in his character might be enormous, these new patterns of action would remain in communication with his past experience (if only as an ongoing criticism of it). We might say that this agent's personal history would include a startling divergence of intention, a reorientation that largely abandons earlier lines of development; but we might also affirm his identity-through-time as a distinct individual agent. It is perhaps impossible to say just how far one might go in this direction without completely disrupting the unity of the agent. These concepts seem to operate rather like a mathematical function that generates a series that infinitely approaches, but never reaches, a specific logical limit. The concept of an agent, that is, admits the possibility of an agent's life pattern being radically reorganized in ways that indefinitely approach, but never reach, complete discontinuity.

The possibility remains, therefore, that an agent who is radically self-creative might reorganize the pattern of his activity in a way that profoundly weakens, but does not destroy, the unity of his life. Will this be a possibility for the life of the divine agent? It appears that it will be unless some additional consideration is introduced.

At this juncture I want to turn to a second line of response to the problem. The notion of radical self-creativity emerged out of experimentation with the thought that God's life might not be founded in any subintentional pattern of activity. This represents an expansion and completion of one of the crucial properties of any agent, namely, the capacity to regulate one's activity intentionally. We now need to explore another way in which agency is brought to perfection in God's life. An agent's effectiveness in determining the content of his own existence is enhanced not only by increasing his capacity to enact his life intentionally, but also by increasing his ability to enact his life as an integrated and coherent whole. We have just seen that the activity of any agent must, to some degree, form an interconnected unity. If God is the perfection of agency, then this "agent-property" also will have its maximal expression in his life: God's life will not only be thoroughly intentional, but also perfectly unified.

Let us develop this point a bit. An agent, we have said, is an enduring individual. But the agent endures only in the sense that he is an integrated and continuous process of change. The identity-through-time of an agent is grounded in the dynamic unity of his life process. An agent is an enduring personal entity (a "self") only insofar as his activity displays a cross-referencing and interdependence that binds it together into the unity of a single life.

If we think of the agent's life in this way, then clearly agent unity admits of degrees. An agent's many projects may be more or less coherent, more or less integrated into an intelligible whole. I commented earlier (in Chap. 5) on the difficulty we have in offering a perceptive assessment of the most significant continuities that appear in our lives as agents; this is due in part to the inherent open-endedness of an agent's life, his capacity for novelty, and it is also due, no doubt, to the limits of our perceptiveness and to our capacity for self-deception. But once this has been acknowledged, more remains to be said. It is often difficult to describe a personal identity because no fully satisfying identity is to be found in an agent's actions. The tendencies at work in a human life are enormously complex, and the integration of these tendencies in any one action is incomplete. A human being's life might be described as an ongoing experiment in harmonizing the diverse claims made upon his action at every moment. As this experiment proceeds from action to action, an agent develops the distinctive style, characteristic interests, enduring attitudes, and so forth that we have in mind in referring to his personal identity. But while this personal identity reflects lines of continuity in the agent's intentional actions, it does not reflect the unity of a single intention. It would be hard to argue convincingly that each of us enacts his life as a single project of great temporal extension and internal variety. Indeed, we rarely if ever enact long stretches of our activity as a single project. The unity that appears in our lives is a unity of many distinct actions that have taken shape in such a way as to be connected with each other in a complex network. This is an "open-textured" unity: our various interests and lines of action often cannot be coordinated in any overarching thematic whole. The unity of a human agent, it appears, is always an unfinished integration of many different kinds and tendencies of activity.

Our experience makes it evident enough that the unity of an agent's life can be confused or disrupted in various ways. The most extreme cases command the greatest fascination: massive loss of memory, startling isolation or "repression" of parts of a person's past experience, eruptions of emotion or action that a person finds both overwhelming and discontinuous with the rest of his behavior, the splitting of a personality into multiple "characters" who are largely out of touch with each other, and so on. But quite apart from these extraordinary disruptions, our lives inevitably include gaps, relative discontinuities, losses of communication with aspects of our own action and experience. This expresses itself in the familiar human experiences of being at odds with oneself, of finding aspects of one's own behavior a mystery, of having to seek self-understanding, of pursuing a well-integrated and durable identity as a goal. All of this points to the incompleteness of the unity that we achieve in our lives. A human agent perpetually tries out new unities and is always both a unity and a disunity, an integration and a dis-integration.

What are we to say of God in this respect? If we understand God as the radicalization and completion of agency, then we will say that God achieves a maximal harmonization of activity in the unity of a single life. God's life will display an undisrupted perfection of agent unity; he will be a self (i.e., a unified individual) in the highest degree. This will not, of course, be a static self-identity. If God is an agent, then he is active, living, perpetually engaged in the enactment of his intentions. All of God's activity, however, will display the closest integration and coherence. His past will not slip from his grasp, but will be taken up and enriched in each of his actions. No part of his experience will be simply abandoned, left outside the integration achieved by each new phase of his activity; rather, all that he has been will be present in the background of each of his actions, and each of his actions will affirm and advance the purposes at work in the projects that preceded it. As a result, there will be no inconstancy in God's action—none of the disillusioned reassessments and sudden reversals that may punctuate the life of a human agent.

Since God is not blind to his own intentions, ignorant of the connections between his actions, or unaware of their possible consequences, he is not confronted with the need to constantly rethink and modify his intentions; rather, he can prescribe the pattern of his life without need for ad hoc modifications of his most fundamental projects. Indeed, it seems correct to say that God's life will display the unity of a single overarching intention. This is not to commit him to an eternity of dull uniformity, since what he intends may admit of unlimited diversity and richness in expression. Given the tremendous range of possibilities for action that are open to him, it is possible for God to be inexhaustibly inventive in realizing his intention. This will be the case, for example, where his actions involve a responsive regard for the actions of his creatures. No restriction can be placed upon God's capacity for novelty of action as he seeks to realize his purposes for the creature without nullifying the creature's purposes for himself. If that intention for the creature includes the creature's fulfillment in relationship with God, then clearly God's intention will embrace an indefinite range of unique particular satisfactions. Though God may will one thing, he can seek to achieve it in an infinite variety of ways. God's unchanging identity of intention will be displayed in an endless creativity of action.

4. INTERLUDE: IS PERFECT UNITY A NECESSARY ATTRIBUTE OF GOD?

We need to pause here for a moment and sort out a particularly tricky set of issues that arise in connection with these claims about the unity of God's life. If has often been claimed that God does not just happen to possess certain properties, but that he could not fail to possess them. I have argued that if we think of God as the perfection of agency, then we must think of God's life as fully unified and harmonious. It is possible to ask, however, whether God must be the perfection of agency. This question does not ask merely for a rule about the use of the term "God"; it will not be enough to stipulate that the term "God" should be applied only to an individual who satisfies the criteria for perfection of agency. In this case the question can immediately arise again in a slightly altered form: Does the agent who in fact satisfies this description *necessarily* satisfy it? Given that an agent satisfies the description "perfection of agency," it is necessary that his life be perfectly unified, but it may not be necessary for that agent to possess that property and thereby satisfy that description. Is it possible for God (taken as the proper name of an agent) to choose not to be "God" (used as the definite description "perfection of agency")?

We can identify at least three significantly different ways of working out a response to this question, one generating an affirmative answer and two generating negative answers. First, one might well argue that unity of action is not a necessary structure in God's life. As a radically self-creative agent, God is (or was) capable of enacting a life of perfect unity, but the exercise of this capacity is strictly an expression of his self-structuring will and is not in any way legislated by his nature. It follows from this, of course, that God might not have enacted a life of perfect unity. But if at any time God was not such a unity, then he never could become one, so if God's life is now fully unified, then it always has been fully unified. This leaves open the possibility, however, that God might choose at some time to revise or abandon his fundamental project and so disrupt the unity of his life. If God's life retains the unity of a single intention, it is because he continuously affirms that intention in each moment of his activity. The unity of God's life will be rooted in the constancy of his will and not in the fixity of his nature.

Second, over against this, one might argue that the properties of God that establish his capacity for a life of perfect unity can be shown to entail that God's life *is* perfectly unified. This represents a purely logical counterclaim to the position I just sketched out. Once again, however, this is not merely to stipulate how the term "God" will be used; rather, it is to take up the concept of God used in stating our initial question and show that it has a logical entailment that rules out the first response I offered. One might argue, for example, that it is impossible to affirm that an agent is radically self-creative, aware of his own intentions and their possible consequences, and confronted by no opposing will, and yet deny that this agent enacts a life of maximal intentional harmony. The burden of argument here lies in showing that an action that would disrupt the unity of this agent's life would not simply be irrational or arbitrary but logically impossible. It must be incoherent to ascribe these properties to God and deny that his life is perfectly unified. If successful, such an argument would allow us to conclude that the very properties that establish God's *capacity* for perfect unity also establish the *logical necessity* of saying that God's life is perfectly unified. This argument would require careful development, however, before we could accurately assess its strength.

Third, one might argue that the mere capacity for disunity is itself a defect that must be denied of God if he is the perfection of agency. In this case one would grant the logical possibility of saying that an agent is capable of a perfectly unified life and yet does not enact such a life, but go on to argue that an agent who could be less than perfectly unified cannot be the perfection of agency even if he chooses a life of perfect unity. An agent must not merely happen to satisfy the description "perfection of agency" by having judiciously exercised his capacity to do so; an agent can only satisfy this description if it is impossible that he have done anything else.[6] Note that the key premise of this argument (viz., that the capacity for disunity is a defect of agency) is weakened if we disassociate "being capable of disunity" from "being susceptible to disunity." If God is able to reorganize his life dramatically, it does not follow that he is in any way "in danger" of doing so. Nonetheless, this argument retains considerable power and might be developed effectively.

Is an argument of this third type compatible with the idea of God as a radically self-creative agent? The argument asserts that living a fully integrated and harmonious life is part of what it is to *be* God. The pattern of God's life is fixed in this respect. If we say this, do we guarantee the unity of God's will at the cost of denying his radical self-creativity?

The concept of a radically self-creative agent was defined in terms of two properties: first, a radically self-creative agent enacts his life without limitation by any subintentional basic life pattern, and second, a radically self-creative agent is free to intend what he will in every relevant sense of the term "free." The proposal that God is necessarily a perfectly unified agent is clearly compatible with the first of these properties. The life of this agent will consist of an undisrupted unity of intentional action. At no point will his activity disappear into a subintentional automatism that grounds and limits his intentional actions. He will enact his life as a unified project.

What are we to say of the freedom of this agent? *Ex hypothesi* he cannot do otherwise than enact a fully unified life pattern. Is this compatible with saying that he is free to intend what he will? At the heart of this question will be a dispute over the sort of freedom that it is important to ascribe to God. Clearly this God *can* be said to be free in some crucial respects. We can claim that his will is not bound by any other agent nor by any circumstance external to his own life. His intentions, including his commitment to unity of action, are not the result of causally sufficient conditions rooted in a subintentional basic life pattern. Insofar as his intentions are necessitated, they are necessitated only by his own nature, by what it is to be God. These senses of "free" seem to be strong enough to allow us to call such an agent "radically self-creative" under the definition I have given for that term. But this freedom is limited in an obvious way: God will not be free to will that his life be disharmonious, that he break with his past, and so on. It is over the value of this freedom for the divine life that the defenders of the first and the third responses to our question will clash.[7] This dispute is at least partly rooted in different theological sensibilities. The first view will emphasize the free fidelity of a God who is at liberty to do otherwise than he has done. Here one may ponder the constancy of the divine will in the face of an infinity of open possibilities. The third view will emphasize the absolute reliability of the divine nature. Here one may point to the immutable foundation of things in a divine will that cannot even be conceived to change.

It is worth noting that precisely these same three patterns of argument will arise in connection with discussion of God's goodness. In his freedom and self-creativity, God is capable of a life of perfect goodness. As he considers possibilities for action, his regard for value will not be diminished or confused by inherent limitations in the scope of his action, by failure to understand his own interests and inclinations, by self-regarding impulses rooted in vulnerability, or the like; rather, he will be able to recognize and act upon the highest values that are relevant to his actions. Indeed, we may decide that any agent who is called "God" must be perfectly good; that is, we may insist that perfect goodness is a necessary condition for being "God" (used as a definite description).

But from this point divergent lines of theological argument may develop. First, we might argue that God (used as a proper name) is capable of perfect goodness but that perfect goodness is not a necessary structure in his life: God could do evil but turns away from it. The utter reliability of God's goodness is an expression of the constancy of his character. Second, against this one might contend that if God is capable of perfect goodness, then he must be perfectly good. Precisely those attributes that make it possible for God to be perfectly good also make it logically necessary that he be perfectly good. The claim that God possesses those attributes and yet is at liberty to do evil would, on this account, be incoherent.[8] Third, one might grant the logical possibility that an agent who is capable of unqualified goodness could nonetheless do evil, and yet one might argue that the liberty to do evil is an imperfection that must be excluded from the life of God. God's perfection requires precisely that he be unable to do evil.

Each of these three proposals about God's unity and goodness involves assumptions and trades upon patterns of inference that become quite complex. Questions about the necessity of the divine attributes are extraordinarily difficult simply as matters of philosophical logic, and claims about the senses in which God might or must be unified and good are freighted with broader theological associations. It is wisest, then, to let these competing positions stand as a rough map of the theological options that open up before us on this issue. For our present purposes, it is not necessary to work out this complex dispute fully. It is enough to recognize that each of these lines of argument could be developed in a way that is compatible with talk of God as an agent; the proposal that God be thought of as the perfection of agency neither begs nor neatly resolves the issues at stake between them.

5. THE POWER OF GOD

We began by developing the idea of an agent whose life is

unrestrictedly intentional, and who therefore enacts his life as his project. We noted that this represents a radicalization of the capacity for self-regulation that any agent must possess in some degree. We then considered a second way in which agency is brought to completion in God—namely, that his life displays a perfection of agent unity. We now turn to a third respect in which God may be said to realize fully the possibilities inherent in the concept of an agent. An agent's powers of action are expanded by increasing the range of actions that it is possible for him to perform. If God is the perfection of agency, then he will have open to him the widest possible scope of action.

The concern to make a claim of this sort, of course, lies at the root of the attribution of omnipotence to God. The principal difficulty here is to fix the range of actions that omnipotence ought to encompass. Any simple assertion that "God can do anything" very quickly runs into trouble. But how much less than "absolutely anything" will constitute a significant content for God's omnipotence? The answer to this question will hinge in part upon what account is given of God's essential attributes. Rather different ways of understanding omnipotence will be generated by each of the three positions I sketched out above in connection with God's unity and goodness. The first and third will disagree about whether God must be granted the capacity to be less than perfectly good and fully unified. The second position will insist that this question cannot meaningfully arise at all.

However these disputes are settled, certain central claims will be common to most forms of theism. Each of the positions I sketched out would assert, for example, that God can achieve whatever he can intend and that God can intend with a range, integration, and effectiveness that exceeds that of any other actual or possible agent. God cannot, of course, set out to create a triangle composed of four intersecting lines: no agent can perform a logically impossible task. And God cannot bring about the deposition of the King of France if in fact there is no King of France, for although the action description "bringing about the deposition of the King of France" is internally consistent, one of the circumstances necessary for its performance does not obtain. This action is logically possible but circumstantially impossible, though God could bring about a circumstance (i.e., the coronation of a King of France) in which the action would be possible.[9] Again, the action "defeating Alaric outside the walls of Rome in 410" is a logically possible project, but it is impossible for any agent after 410. Or once again, Oedipus can, but God cannot, kill his father and marry his mother. There are some actions that can be performed only by agents of a particular type. One could go on spinning out qualifications that must be placed upon the range of actions that it is possible for God to intend, but the fundamental claim involved in the ascription of omnipotence to God is clear: God faces no limitation upon his activity that is not either logically or circumstantially necessary.

Of greater theological interest than the project of unpacking all of the qualifications this general formula entails, is the observation that an omnipotent agent cannot confront any given network of objects and agents (i.e., a world) the presence of which imposes limits upon the range of projects open to him. A finite agent's scope of action is ordinarily shaped and limited by the world of others with which he interacts. He may be capable of recognizing a wide range of possibilities for action within his field of interaction, and he may have considerable freedom to respond creatively to that world, but inevitably his life unfolds as a pattern of interaction with an environment that confronts his intentions with its all-too-unyielding demands. The finite agent belongs to a world which is the natural and supportive context of his life, but which is also a limiting structure that resists his intentions and is always able to destroy him. There is a givenness not only at the foundation of his own activity but also in the structure of his world.

I have already noted that it is important to a theist to claim that God exists noncontingently, or independently; that is, God's continued existence is not dependent upon his relation to other beings. But this alone does not rule out the possibility that God may confront a given network of objects and agents with which he is bound to interact. In that case God's life will necessarily take shape as a pattern of interaction structured not only by his own intentions, but also by the properties and powers of the beings that impinge upon his activity. At the very least it will not be open to God to structure his life as a pattern of activity without interaction. God may be unrestrictedly intentional in his activity, but if he faces a given network of relationships, then the range of actions open to him will not be unrestricted. Though God intends all that he is, what he intends will be shaped and limited by the world he confronts.

If, therefore, we wish to speak of God as an agent who faces no restriction upon his activity that is not either necessary or self-imposed, we must deny that God finds himself confronting a given network of interaction; rather, God will have no world unless he brings one into being and sustains it in existence. His life need not include a pattern of relationship with other agents, though it can take this form if he chooses to structure it in this way. This is not to say that God must perpetually exist in a barren (or even magnificent) solitude. Nor is it to say that God must at some time have existed without others. God may always have had a world, this being the pattern he has intended for his life eternally. But if we say that God has no given framework of interaction, then we say that he is capable of existing without others and that he can give his life a content over and above his creative and providential relation to creatures. Though God chooses to be with and for others, and though he may always intend and enact this relation, he may nonetheless establish a basic pattern for his life that transcends his relation to creatures. His life need not be exhaustively identified with his activity as the source of life for others.

Having said this, we do not bar God from entering fully and sympathetically into mutually affecting relations with creatures. There is no conceptual barrier to ascribing to God both the capacity to be without others and the capacity to be eminently in relationship with others. God's life may lack no richness without the creature, and yet he may choose to concern himself with others—indeed, to engage creatures with a love that penetrates to the very center of each individual's life and coincides with the act that sustains that individual's existence.

In establishing this relation to creatures, God commits himself to a pattern of interaction that qualifies the scope and direction of his activity. He creates a field of other agents whose integrity he respects and so whose independent actions condition his choices. This amounts to a purposeful limitation of the scope of his own activity, but it does not nullify his omnipotence: he remains an all-powerful and radically self-creative agent capable of freely regulating his own pattern of life at every moment of his existence. Intentional self-restraint does not represent a renunciation of omnipotence, but rather a renunciation of certain uses of power, and this is entirely in keeping with God's unlimited self-creativity.

A question arises here as to whether a radically self-creative and omnipotent agent might irrevocably limit the scope of his own action. Might God intentionally set events in motion that thereafter are binding upon him, immune to modification in the future? This question bears a deceptive resemblance to a classic dilemma and arch example of theological reflection gone haywire. When a critic wishes to illustrate the bankruptcy of the excessively curious theological intellect, he can always point to one of its embarrassing products, such as the question "Can God create a stone so heavy that he cannot lift it?" The question is obviously silly and the illustration inevitably persuasive. But the issue raised by the question does possess some significance. Alvin Plantinga sets out the problem in the form of a dilemma:

> (1) Either God can make things He cannot control or God cannot make things He cannot control.
> (2) If He can, then if He did, He would not be omnipotent.
> (3) If He cannot, then there are things He cannot do and hence He is not omnipotent.[10]

This dilemma would force on us the conclusion that the concept of an omnipotent agent cannot be formed at all.

It is hard not to feel that a verbal trick has been played here, and in fact it appears that one has. The dilemma can be dismantled by taking a closer look at the third move. We are asked to grant that if God cannot create things he cannot control, then he is not omnipotent. The first clause of this conditional is the denial of an inability ("God cannot create things he cannot control"). We can eliminate the double negative by saying, "Any being God creates, God can control." But now it should be evident how odd it is to claim that this is a limitation upon the scope of God's action, for this is part of what we *mean* by saying that God is all-powerful. The ascription of omnipotence cannot, when expressed as a denial of inability, be considered a genuine limitation upon God's ability to act.

It might be considered a limitation upon God's ability to act, however, if we were to deny that God, in his omnipotence, could divest himself of his omnipotence. One might argue that an omnipotent being must have the power to limit his power irrevocably. This, however, is not to say that the omnipotent being creates beings he cannot control; rather, it is to say that he so modifies *himself* that he is no longer omnipotent and *therefore* there will be things he cannot control. The crucial question here is whether the action of intentionally limiting one's capacity to act intentionally is a logically possible action for a radically self-creative agent, for in the life of such an agent, the capacity for intentional action is not rooted in any given basic pattern that might be intentionally disrupted. It appears that the action of irrevocable self-limitation would have to be a basic action for this peculiar agent. But we may wonder whether it makes sense to say that the action of depriving oneself of a capacity for action can itself be a basic action, just as we previously wondered whether the action of acquiring a capacity for action can itself be a basic action. We need not decide this question here, however, for in either case no problem is posed for talk of divine omnipotence. If this action cannot be coherently ascribed to this agent, then his "inability" to perform it cannot represent a limitation upon his powers of action. If the capacity for irreversible self-limitation can be coherently ascribed to God, it is in any case perfectly compatible with his omnipotence so long as he does not exercise it.

Omnipotence, in the sense I have given to this term, requires that the omnipotent agent have no world of interaction unless he creates one. Such an agent may have eternally maintained a relation to creatures, but it must be possible that he have existed without them. Can we, however, make sense of intentional action without interaction or of an agent without a network of others that his actions engage? It is hard to envision agency in a void, action that never makes "contact," that seeks no result from a field of entities distinct from the agent. The idea of an agent whose actions do not unfold within a framework of interaction suggests a spare, restricted, even dismal existence to us. The richness of our lives comes not from our limited capacity to act without interaction, but from action that engages our world, both natural and social. Our lives are always placed in a field of vital interests in which our existence is both sustained and threatened and apart from which we cannot envision a content for our lives. But all this, of course, expresses the particular nature of our existence as human agents and does not, without some further argument, represent a requirement binding upon the life of every agent.

It is not at all obvious that the idea of action without interaction is nonsensical. As we have seen, the concept of intentional action is the logical concomitant of the concept of an agent. The concept "agent" that we have been working with is the concept of an operative unit capable of intentionally structuring its own activity. The agent's action, then, is a segment of activity undertaken as a unit defined by the "rule" (the action description) that the agent adopts for that activity. There is nothing in this that entails that an agent's actions must engage a network of entities distinct from the agent. We do, in fact, perform actions that do not intend any interaction with others, though these actions always take place in a broader context of active concern with our field of interaction.

If God were to exist as an agent without others, then his projects would be projects strictly for his own activity. His action would be the enactment of his pattern of existence—a pattern that would not, in this case, involve interaction with creatures. Unpreoccupied with the contingencies of a given world, the divine agent's activity would concern strictly the realization and enjoyment of possibilities for his own activity, like a song sung solely for the satisfaction that the singer takes in its inherent beauty. God, of course, does not exist without creatures. He chooses to sing his song for creatures and to call out of creatures whatever responsive melody they can manage. But if God's life also transcends his life with creatures, then part of its content will be enjoyed by himself alone.

The life of God apart from the creature is obviously something about which the theologian cannot be expected to have much to say. The pattern of active existence that God enacts as his own can be characterized only insofar as it appears in and through the relation he establishes to creatures. It is interesting to observe that for Christian theological reflection this representation of the divine life on the basis of God's dealings with us has taken a trinitarian form. Trinitarian theology suggests that God's life is structured as a pattern of differentiation and relationship. God is in relation not only by virtue of being the creator of other agents, but also by virtue of the pattern of life he establishes independent of his dealings with creatures. It is at this point that a traditional Christian doctrine of God may have to struggle with questions about oneness and manyness, identity and internal differentiation, that are parallel to the questions posed for an organismic theology in thinking about the divine agent and his creaturely constituents.

CONCLUSION

In this and the preceding chapter I have sketched the outline of three theological proposals, differentiated in terms of their response to the question about divine embodiment. Each of these proposals faces its own peculiar difficulties as a development of the concept of an agent. All three could be further elaborated and refined. But the proposal that God be thought of as the unembodied perfection of agency seems to be the most useful theologically. At the same time, it does not appear to pose conceptual problems more difficult than those presented by either of the other two proposals.

I have argued that if we conceive of God as the perfection of agency, then we will say that God is a radically self-creative agent whose life displays a perfect unity of intention and who is the omnipotent creator of all other beings. There is a great deal more that we will want to say about God, of course, but this provides fundamental conceptual structures that can organize further theological reflection. If we say that agency is brought to perfection in God's life, then we have a logically individuating description that sets the terms to be followed in developing a doctrine of God. There can in principle be only one agent who acts with unqualified creativity—that is, who is both radically self-creative and omnipotent—for this agent will not only freely establish the basic pattern of his own life, but will also establish the network of his relationships with others. Any agent with whom he interacts must have been created by him and continue to exist only because he intends that agent's existence.

Like all logically individuating descriptions, this one gives us relatively little information about the individual who satisfies it. While we may take this as an appropriate specification of what we mean by "God," it does not tell us *who* God is. We are provided with an abstract description of a form of agency—a form that can be filled by just one individual but that might, *ex hypothesi*, be filled by that individual in any of an indefinite number of ways. An identification of God through the unique mode of his agency will not take on the concreteness of a description of personal identity until we say something about what God has chosen to be, how he has given shape to his life in action. Here we reach the outer boundary of my project in this essay: a philosophical theology that identifies God as the perfection of agency points beyond itself to a doctrinal theology that reflects upon the content and character of God's acts.

Theistic religious traditions do not, of course, begin with this formal identification of an agent and then ask how this form is in fact filled out in the life of God. The Christian and the Jew live under the influence of a rich complex of ideas and practices that define their theism as a way of life, a focus for imagination, emotion, reflection, and action. It is only because this religious life-structure gives a prominent place to images of God as intending and acting that theological reflection is led to the conceptual form "the perfection of agency." This abstract idea represents one way of systematically articulating the skeletal conceptual structure at work in the language and practice of theism.

Needless to say, there are other ways of establishing the conceptual groundwork for theological construction. It may be helpful to set this theistic proposal in relation to two other prominent (and mutually antagonistic) options—process theology and classical (in this case Thomistic) theism. My purpose is to sketch briefly some patterns of similarity and difference, rather than to offer a decisive analysis and critique; the issues at work in evaluating these competing conceptual schemes are too complex to air thoroughly here. I do want to suggest, however, that conceiving of God as the perfection of agency opens up a path between process theology and classical theism, and nicely balances some of their contrasting strengths and weaknesses. It is also the case, of course, that neither the process theologian nor the classical theist is likely to be satisfied with this proposal.

One of the most common modern criticisms of classical theism leveled by process theologians and others is that it fails to do justice to the deeply embedded tendency in Christian self-expression to represent God as a personal power who engages persons in dynamic interaction. Part of what is at stake in this complaint is a disagreement about what it is to "do justice" to these aspects of Christian religious language. That dispute is not easily resolved. But it is easy enough to recognize the grounds for worry about the classical treatment of personalistic themes in Christian discourse. Thomas Aquinas's account of the personal, or moral, attributes of God illustrates the point. For Thomas, personal attributes like love, wisdom, mercy, and so on, are understood as perfections of being; that is, the act of existing (*esse*) is more fully expressed in a being who possesses these perfections than in one who does not. Because these perfections reflect the creature's positive participation in being, they will have a transcendent correlate in Being-itself (*ipsum esse*). As being rises up the scale of perfection toward unlimited plentitude, these perfections will approach their fullest possible expression.

At this point, however, we encounter the source of difficulty, for in the absolute simplicity of Being-itself, all perfection is one; here the diverse perfections we identify in creatures lose their distinctness and are fused in the undifferentiated unity of pure actuality.[11] This primordial perfection of being, however, lies beyond the reach of our concepts of love, wisdom, justice, mercy, and so on, for these are concepts of nonidentical properties; we cannot assert their identity without breaking down the rules of use that define them. The result is that God is not an instance of any concept such as "love" or "justice" that we possess: we do not know what it means to say that God is loving because we do not know what it is to be *ipsum esse*.[12] Nonetheless, these predicates can and must be applied to God precisely because, as *ipsum esse*, he is the essential expression of every perfection of being.[13] God is the ultimate ground of the personal perfections that appear as enhancements of the being of creatures, but in God these perfections are reabsorbed into the suprapersonal unity of absolute Being. If we can say that certain personal attributes are brought to perfection in God's being, it seems equally appropriate to say that they are so utterly transformed as to disappear altogether.

Process theologians, for all the variety in their particular views, join forces in arguing the theological inadequacy of this metaphysic of pure Being. Over against the impassive perfection of the God of Thomistic metaphysics, they insist upon God's intimate and interactive relation to creatures. Charles Hartshorne, for example, has argued vigorously that if we are to ascribe personal perfections to God we must deny that God's relation to creatures is strictly "external" (i.e., that this relation affects creatures but does not affect God). If God is to be worthy of *moral* admiration, Hartshorne argues, then he must be open to the creature's influence.[14] On this account, God's perfection consists precisely in the perfection of his capacity for sympathetic appropriation of every creature's experience and loving involvement with every creature's destiny.

Beyond affirming that the content of God's experience and the direction of his activity are affected by the experience and activity of creatures, process theologians characteristically insist that God's life necessarily consists of relation to creatures. This claim takes significantly different forms in different process theologies, but the fundamental idea is a consistent and identifying mark of process thought: to be a distinct center of experience and action is to be a creative integration of relations to other centers of experience and action. God is no exception to this general metaphysical principle: he could not exist without a world of others. God's distinctiveness consists, most simply, in (a) the perfect scope and depth of his relatedness to others and (b) the preeminence of his creative influence upon the world process in accordance with his primordial ordering of values. God is related as fully as possible to every individual, and he contributes in a crucial way to the orientation of each individual's own self-creativity. But he does not choose to stand in this universally receptive and contributory relation to others; rather, his being as God consists in this relation.

There is no question, then, of God creating other beings *ex nihilo*. God and the world are coeternal and mutually dependent. As Whitehead put it in the concluding lines of a well-known passage from *Process and Reality*, "It is as true to say that God creates the World, as that the World creates God. God and the World are the contrasted opposites in terms of which Creativity achieves its supreme task of transforming disjoined multiplicity, . . . into concrescent unity."[15] The creature creates God insofar as the creature's self-determination shapes what it becomes and so shapes the contribution it makes to God's experience. God creates the creature insofar as he determines the initial possibility, which the creature then pursues in its own self-determining way.[16] Given this crucial role in the life of every individual, God is the supremely creative agent in the universe. But God's creativity does not account for the being of finite individuals (i.e., for the fact *that* they are); rather, it accounts for the initial orientation of their becoming (i.e., for a crucial ingredient in *what* they are). God's life, then, is lived out at the center of a creative process that transcends and includes him. Creative becoming—that is, the novel integration of relation to others in the unity of each individual's experience—is the fundamental metaphysical fact for Whitehead. God does not account for this fact;

rather, he preeminently exemplifies it. God is an instance, not the ultimate origin, of the creative becoming that characterizes our world.[17]

The proposal that I introduce in this chapter represents a third option, and in certain respects a mediating alternative to both these competing conceptual schemes and theological sensibilities. If we conceive of God as the perfection of agency, then we will join classical theism in affirming that God is the ontological creator of all finite beings. If God is radically self-creative and omnipotent, then he will be the ultimate (though *not*, if he so chooses, the exclusive) ground of all creativity. God will exist from himself (*a se*) in sovereign independence from the world of creatures. His creative activity will not only be supremely influential in shaping the direction of creaturely activity, but will also continually sustain the being of creatures. In this respect, the proposal that God be thought of as the perfection of agency breaks sharply with process theology.

In other respects, however, this proposal shares important theological concerns with process thought, for it emphasizes personalistic categories in the doctrine of God and allows for mutually affecting relations between God and creatures. Though God can exist without creatures, he can also freely call them into being as finite centers of self-creativity whose choices condition his own. As the perfection of agency, God is characterized by sovereign freedom: freedom to be what he is without relation to creatures, and freedom to commit himself to creatures as finite co-creatures whose integrity he respects. God does not have his being in essential relatedness to creatures, but neither is his ontological independence linked to an immutable self-containment that excludes the possibility of internal relation to finite beings. In his creative activity, God enters into a relationship with creatures that both grounds each creature's existence at every moment and appreciates that creature's experience from its very center. And if God "lets us go out of his hand" in the exercise of a limited self-creativity, then he commits himself to an interactive relationship in which our decisions help set the conditions for the realization of his purposes.[18] The perfect unity of God's intention for his creation will then be worked out in an ongoing (and inexhaustibly inventive) response to his creature's diverse intentions for themselves.

On this account, we not only identify God abstractly through the unique form of his agency but we can also give at least a limited description of how God fills out this form. When we speak about what God has done and is doing, we move beyond a merely conceptual identification of God as the perfection of agency and point toward the particular content God has given his life in action. This sets up an interesting contrast with classical theism. The classical theist can identify God through the unique form of God's being (i.e., as *ipsum esse*), but he cannot say what it is to be God. Our descriptive vocabulary (including our vocabulary of personal attributes) is ordered to the representation of particular beings, and cannot be extended to Being-itself without inadvertently reducing it to a peculiar instance of being. Hence, though God is the ground of personal existence, his being transcends personal categories. If God is understood as the perfection of agency, however, he will possess a distinctive personal identity constituted in the continuities of purpose and character that bind his activity together. Where God's activity is encountered and acknowledged, this distinctive identity will be revealed. As with other agents, we will be able to give an account of *who* God is on the basis of what he does.

Here at the end of our discussion, therefore, we return to the topic with which we began, namely, the use of character trait predicates in describing the personal identity of an agent. If God is an agent, then we will be able to ascribe these distinctively personal attributes to him quite straightforwardly. In saying that God is loving, we are not saying that the love we recognize in creatures has an unknown metaphysical counterpart within the simple perfection of God's being; rather, we are saying that God loves in the concrete ways displayed in his actions and that these actions faithfully represent God's identity as an agent. Insofar as God's actions fall under the informal criteria that govern the use of terms like "loving," "just," and "wise," these character trait predicates can be applied to him just as "literally" as they are applied to persons. None of the rules that we have noted for the use of these predicates need be modified in order to ascribe them to a divine agent on the basis of his intentional actions.

It does not follow from this, however, that God's love (for example) is no different in quality, no greater, purer, or more inclusive than the most exalted human love. We have already seen that character trait predicates can be used to appraise a tremendous range of quite diverse actions. A predicate such as "loving" or "patient" or "wise" does not pick out an identical quality in each action, but rather calls attention to a complex network of likenesses among actions. These predicates are capable of an indefinite variety of expression in particular actions and in the lives of different agents. The specific quality that a character trait predicate identifies in an agent will vary with the pattern of action in which that attribute appears. The divine perfections, therefore, are not somehow reduced to merely human traits by being characterized in the evaluative language we use to appraise human agents; they remain the distinctive properties of an agent whose mode of life and powers of action differ fundamentally from our own. If the scope and content of God's action is unique, then so too will be the character of his love or patience or wisdom.

Not only will God's personal attributes be unique to him alone, but they will inevitably exceed our capacity to describe them. This failure of understanding, however, is not the result of a fundamental inapplicability of our concepts to the divine being; rather, our understanding of God's personal attributes is limited because our understanding of his actions and intentions is limited. Insofar as our knowledge of what an agent (*any* agent) intends is incomplete, it is difficult to form a thorough understanding of his identity. I have already mentioned the difficulties attending our efforts to comprehend the agents we ought by all rights to understand best, namely, one another. These difficulties are vastly magnified when the individual we seek to understand radically transcends the mode and scope of our own activity. We cannot expect to describe God's actions fully since they are not possible actions for us; his range and power of action is unique. He entertains an array of possibilities that includes but vastly outreaches those that we can comprehend. His intentions in the actions we attribute to him will extend far beyond our description of those intentions—indeed, beyond the range of any project we have the power to envision. The particular divine actions we identify will be rooted within a project of enormous scope, embracing the whole of our world in a single intention. As a result, the full content of God's life, and therefore the full character of his love or wisdom, cannot but escape our grasp.

It is important to note that this ignorance of God that accompanies our knowledge of him is not merely a regrettable accident;

knowledge and ignorance are inseparably bound together in this instance. Our knowledge of God's personal attributes rests upon our understanding of his actions: in those divine actions that engage us and awaken a recognition of their agent we are given access to the distinctive content of God's life. Insofar as we can describe God's actions at all we can ascribe character trait predicates on the basis of those actions and so illuminate the personal identity of their agent. It is precisely by pointing to divine actions that we are able to give a specific meaning to our ascription of love or wisdom to God. We can, that is, indicate at least something of the special *way* in which God is loving or wise by describing what we believe him to have done. No sooner is this said, however, than we must pair with it an acknowledgment of the limits of our understanding. The human imagination, rooted in our limited life pattern, cannot adequately represent the activity of the divine agent. We can catch a glimpse of God's life in his dealings with us, but our understanding of his identity as an agent will be unavoidably provisional and incomplete. The necessary concomitant of ascribing love or wisdom to God is admitting our fundamental inability fully to spell out how these perfections are expressed in his life. However confident we may be that God does make himself known in action, the divine agent will remain a mystery that radically transcends us.

If we conceive of God as the perfection of agency, therefore, we can both allow for a positive knowledge of God's attributes and explain why our knowledge must be accompanied by ignorance, our comprehension by incomprehension. Working with these resources, it is the task of a fuller doctrinal theology to reflect upon God's acts, and so display that knowledge of God which stands out against our ignorance.

Notes

INTRODUCTION

1. Augustine, *The Confessions of St. Augustine,* trans. Rex Warner (New York: New American Library, 1963), pp. 135-36.

2. Ibid., p. 137.

3. Ibid., pp. 18-19.

4. One result of emphasizing these categories is to open up a way of thinking about God that is neither purely "classical" nor "neo-classical" but that marks out a fruitful alternative to these opposing patterns of theological construction. See Chapters 6-7 (especially the concluding section of Chap. 7).

5. Karl Barth, *Church Dogmatics,* trans T. H. L. Parker *et al.* (Edinburgh: T. & T. Clark, 1957), vol. 2, *The Doctrine of God,* pt. 1; Charles Hartshorne, *Man's Vision of God* (New York: Harper & Row, 1941), and *The Divine Relativity: A Social Conception of God* (New Haven: Yale University Press, 1948); Austin Farrer, *Faith and Speculation* (New York: New York University Press, 1967).

6. See, for example, G. Ernest Wright, *God Who Acts: Biblical Theology as Recital* (London: SCM Press, 1952); G. Ernest Wright and Reginald H. Fuller, *The Book of the Acts of God* (Garden City, N.Y.: Doubleday, 1957); and B. Anderson, *Understanding the Old Testament* (Englewood Cliffs, N.J.: Prentice-Hall, 1957).

7. On difficulties with the claim of biblical theologians to have captured *the* biblical view, see James Barr's *The Semantics of Biblical Language* (London: Oxford University Press, 1961). On the complexities of warranting theological proposals by appeal to Scripture, see David H. Kelsey's *The Uses of Scripture in Recent Theology* (Philadelphia: Fortress Press, 1975).

8. Langdon Gilkey, "Cosmology, Ontology, and the Travail of Biblical Language," *Journal of Religion,* 41 (1961): 194-205.

9. Wright, *God Who Acts,* chap. 5.

10. Schubert Ogden, *The Reality of God* (New York: Harper & Row, 1963), chap. 6; Gordon Kaufman, *God the Problem* (Cambridge: Harvard University Press, 1972), chaps. 3, 4, 6.

11. Ogden, *Reality of God,* p. 177. This language is difficult to interpret. It seems to involve a fusion of (early) Heideggerian themes with the Whiteheadian idea that every real individual (actual entity) is a partially self-determining integration of relations to other individuals.

12. Ibid.

13. Ibid., p. 179.

14. Ibid., p. 177.

15. Kaufman, *God the Problem,* p. 63.

16. Ibid., pp. 120-25, 129-35.

17. Ibid., p. 137. On the distinction between master act and sub-acts, see p. 136.

18. This point has been noted by a number of commentators on Ogden. See, for example, James McClendon's "Can There Be Talk about God-and-the-World?" *Harvard Theological Review,* 62 (1969): 45-46, n. 12; and David Kelsey's "Can God Be Agent without Body?" *Interpretation,* 27 (1973): 358-62.

19. See my comments in notes 6 and 8 to Chapter 6 of this text on the difference between mind-body dualism and Whiteheadian talk of the mind as an enduring entity distinct from the body.

20. F. Michael McLain, "On Theological Models," *Harvard Theological Review,* 62 (1969): 155-87. Kaufman responds to McLain's criticisms in the Preface to *God the Problem.* I discuss Kaufman's proposals at greater length in Chap. 3, pp. 128-31 and Chap. 4, n. 24.

21. Paul Edwards, "Difficulties in the Idea of God," in *The Idea of God: Philosophical Perspectives,* ed. Edward Madden, Rollo Handy, and Marvin Farber (Springfield: Charles C. Thomas, 1968), p. 48. See also Edwards, "Some Notes on Anthropomorphic Theology," in *Religious Experience and Truth,* ed. Sydney Hook (New York: New York University Press, 1961); Kai Nielson, *Contemporary Critiques of Religion* (New York: Herder and Herder, 1971), pp. 119-28; and T. Penelhum, *Survival and Disembodied Existence* (London: Routledge & Kegan Paul, 1970), chap. 10.

22. W. D. Hudson, *A Philosophical Approach to Religion* (London: Macmillan, 1974), p. 173.

CHAPTER 1

1. It is worth noting that this "agent-as-subject" requirement is not a *sufficient* condition for counting a predicate as a trait of character. Ascriptions of intentional action satisfy this requirement. And a plausible argument can be made that "states of consciousness" (e.g., perceptions, feelings, thoughts) require that any subject to which they are ascribed be an agent of intentional actions (see Stuart Hampshire's *Thought and Action* [London: Chatto & Windus, 1959], chap. 1). But neither intentional actions nor states of consciousness fit the rough categories I have used to identify traits of character. One could define a class of predicates that demands only that the agent-as-subject requirement be satisfied as the necessary *and* sufficient condition for inclusion. This would resemble the class that Peter Strawson refers to as "P-predicates," though it would probably be somewhat narrower in scope (P. F. Strawson, *Individuals: An Essay in Descriptive Metaphysics*

[Garden City, N.Y.: Doubleday-Anchor, 1963], pp. 100ff.). In any case, if we call this broader group of predicates (defined simply by the agent-as-subject requirement) the class of person-predicates, then we can say that the task of this chapter is to show that the class of person-predicates will at least include all traits of character.

2. It would be odd, of course, to speak of ascribing a trait of character to an action. The predicates that I am discussing are used as traits of character only when ascribed to individuals (e.g., persons) rather than when used to evaluate behaviors. I have taken the class name from the former use.

3. Gilbert Ryle, *The Concept of Mind* (New York: Barnes & Noble, 1949), chap. 5.

4. Ibid., p. 123.

5. Ibid., p. 43.

6. I am using the term *behavior* here to indicate not only the intentional and unintentional actions of persons, but also the motions, changes of state, and so on of objects. This, I believe, conforms to Ryle's own usage, and repeats a crucial ambiguity in his account of dispositional properties, an ambiguity that I will discuss in section 4 of this chapter.

Ryle does try to tighten up this rough definition of a dispositional property. He argues throughout *The Concept of Mind* that statements ascribing dispositional properties to individuals entail (and perhaps are equivalent to) certain "law-like hypothetical propositions" (p. 89). The paradigmatic case of a hypothetical proposition is an *if-then* statement correlating certain behaviors with certain observable circumstances, such as "If this object is struck with a force of magnitude 'x', then it will shatter." The ascription of a dispositional property is *law-like* because, while it does assert the applicability of certain circumstance-behavior correlations, the range of application asserted for these correlations is too limited for them to count as general laws (pp. 120-25). A dispositional statement asserts that certain generalizations hold for the behavior of this or that individual (and for all other individuals to which the predicate can be ascribed) over some period of time. During the period of applicability of these generalizations we can predict behavior in accordance with them and explain past or present behavior as belonging to these larger regularities (p. 124).

This appeal to the notion of a law-like hypothetical proposition allows Ryle to define the technical notion "dispositional property" with considerable precision. It also threatens to generate a reductive behaviorism that exhaustively translates the meaning of statements ascribing, say, generosity or wit or vanity into sets of circumstance-behavior correlations. If Ryle avoids this behaviorism, it is largely because he qualifies his use of the empirical law analogy for dispositional properties. He does so at two points in particular. First, the circumstance-behavior correlations that express the content of a dispositional property cannot, for many properties, be specified in detail. It is precisely in considering certain traits of character that Ryle recognizes this. He tells us, for example, that the pride that characterizes the heroine of *Pride and Prejudice* eludes complete expression in any manageable set of circumstance-behavior generalizations (p. 44). The attempt to give a full account of the propositional content of the dispositional property "pride" in any particular instance would commit us to "an infinite series of different hypothetical propositions" (p. 44).

Second, the probability of the behavior correlated with a particular circumstance occurring when that circumstance obtains will vary with different types of dispositions. At one point Ryle distinguishes between capacities and tendencies, for example, in terms of the probability of the behavior-circumstance correlations that constitute them. "Roughly, to say 'can' is to say that it is not a certainty that something will not be the case, while to say 'tends', 'keeps on' or 'is prone', is to say that it is a good bet that it will be, or was, the case" (p. 131). When we say that Jones can change a tire, we are saying that given a flat, it cannot be ruled out that Jones will change a tire (see pp. 126ff.). This is surely an odd and incomplete account of capacities, and it is only one of several rather disparate things Ryle has to say on this topic (see, for example, his discussion of "competence to follow instructions" on p. 129). It illustrates, however, Ryle's introduction of multiple probabilities into his account of the hypothetical generalizations that constitute dispositional properties. Not only do we have the high-probability *if-then* correlations of the paradigmatic case, but also the *if-then likely* correlations of a tendency and the *if-then it cannot be ruled out* correlations of some capacities.

Dispositional statements, then, will vary not only in the behavior to which they call attention, but also in the degree to which the behavior that satisfies them can be specified, the degree to which it is possible to specify just what counts as an "appropriate occasion" for the display of that behavior, and the probability of the requisite behavior occurring on these appropriate occasions. These concessions to the diversity of dispositional properties considerably qualify Ryle's original claim that statements ascribing such properties bear a significant likeness to generalizations that might count as "laws." The strongest general statement we can now make about the hypothetical form of dispositional statements is that every dispositional statement will assert that there is some probability that behavior of a certain sort (viz., behavior that can be appraised by the dispositional property in question) will occur on appropriate occasions. This certainly removes the threat of an unwanted behaviorism that might otherwise have attached itself to Ryle's use of the notion of law-like hypothetical propositions, but it also leaves him with a definition of dispositional properties that is so accommodatingly vague as to be unilluminating.

7. Compare A. I. Melden, *Free Action* (London: Routledge & Kegan Paul, 1961), chap. 2, "Character and Causal Circumstance."

8. Ryle recognizes that and makes a distinction between *determinate* and *determinable* dispositions (*Concept of Mind*, pp. 44, 118). A determinate disposition has a relatively specific set of possible exercises. The fragile object breaks; the smoker smokes. By contrast, a determinable disposition (e.g., generosity) can be exercised in a wide range of different particular actions.

9. This seems to signal a difference in senses of "disposition." A dispositional property such as "fragility" points out a susceptibility to behavior of a certain type under certain conditions. A dispositional property such as "generosity" picks out a pattern of frequently displayed behavior. In the one case it is necessary for appropriate ascription of the dispositional property only that a subject will display behavior "x" on condition "y." In the other case, it is necessary to have displayed the behavior in question with some

frequency. There is clearly a stronger and a weaker sense of "disposition" here. The stronger demands that a particular individual has displayed and/or will display certain behaviors. The weaker demands that certain behaviors would be displayed if certain conditions are realized.

10. *Concept of Mind,* p. 86.

11. Ibid., p. 89.

12. This is not to claim that all behavior will fit neatly into one of the two categories "intentional action" and "something that merely happens," however; rather, it is to claim only that an irreducible distinction is to be drawn between cases that do clearly fit one of these descriptions. There are a tremendous number of behaviors that are ambiguous with regard to this distinction, such as the "instinctual" behavior of many living organisms, a person's inadvertent mannerisms, and so on. The distinction between *action* and *happening* is useful only in indicating two poles of a scale and not in identifying exhaustive alternatives. The chief point to be made in this discussion is that if we are to ascribe traits of character, we must allow such a distinction and not restrict the terms of discussion to happenings that appear in patterns of varying complexity.

13. *Concept of Mind,* p. 40.

14. In section 4 of Chapter 5 I discuss in greater detail the intended and unintended continuities of action that constitute character.

15. *Concept of Mind,* p. 138. Ryle distrusts the attempt to draw a general distinction between action and happening, but he is explicitly concerned, nonetheless, to distinguish what a person does on purpose from (a) what he does accidentally or automatically, and (b) what he suffers or undergoes. See, for example, p. 74 for a distinction between what a person does (intentionally or unintentionally) and what just happens; see pp. 40 and 126 on behaviors that display qualities of intellect as opposed to behaviors attributable to reflex, blind impulse, or absence of mind; see p. 132 on "pure habit" versus purposive action; and see pp. 33 and 145-46 on doing something "on purpose."

16. *Concept of Mind,* p. 140; see also p. 139.

17. Ibid., p. 141.

18. Ibid., pp. 142-43.

19. It is not correct, however, to say that "Jones is trying to keep the deer out of his cornfield" entails "Jones is building a fence around his corn," "Jones is out shooting deer," or "Jones is blindfolding every deer he can catch." Any or all of these statements might be false and the assertion about Jones be true. Stuart Hampshire has justifiably accused Ryle of mixing entailment patterns and characteristic truth conditions in his account of dispositional properties ("Critical Review of *The Concept of Mind,*" in *Ryle: A Collection of Critical Essays,* ed. Oscar Wood and George Pitcher [Garden City, N.Y.: Doubleday-Anchor, 1970]).

20. See, for example, his discussion of playing chess, *Concept of Mind,* p. 140.

21. *Concept of Mind,* p. 28, quoted in n. 22, following.

22. Cf. Robert King's discussion of Ryle in *The Meaning of God* (Philadelphia: Fortress Press, 1973), pp. 38-40. King notes the distinction between action and occurrence, and suggests that Ryle tends to equate the two. This happens, King argues, because Ryle's dispositional analysis takes the point of

view of an observer as opposed to that of the agent.

This assessment of Ryle is parallel to my own. It is important to note, however, that being an observer in no way commits one to treating another's behavior as mere happening. An observer of agents will witness intentional actions. Ryle's claim that intentional-action language displays a dispositional logic is important and need not lead to behaviorism. The central problem with Ryle's discussion is his inability or unwillingness to clarify the distinction between the disposition of an agent to undertake actions that realize his intention and the disposition of an object to undergo certain changes under particular conditions. Though Ryle fails to shed much light on this distinction, he does not deny it. Note for example the following striking passage from *The Concept of Mind:* "The well-regulated clock keeps good time and the well-drilled circus seal performs its tricks flawlessly, yet we do not call them 'intelligent'. We reserve this title for the persons responsible for their performances. To be intelligent is not merely to satisfy criteria, but to apply them; to regulate one's actions and not merely to be well-regulated" (p. 28).

23. *Concept of Mind,* p. 140.

24. Ibid., pp. 120-25.

CHAPTER 2

1. See Stuart Hampshire's *Thought and Action* (London: Chatto and Windus, 1959), pp. 193-94, and Gilbert Ryle's *The Concept of Mind* (New York: Barnes & Noble, 1949), chap. 2.

2. Note that the instrumental relation of "performing action A_1 in order to perform A_2" is not in every case based upon a causal relation of the events involved in A_1 to those involved in A_2. The action "throwing the ball" does bear a causal relation to "putting the ball through the hoop," but the further action "making a basket" is not, strictly speaking, an event caused by the action "putting the ball through the hoop"; rather, "putting the ball through the hoop" counts as "making a basket" when the rules of the game of basketball are applied in appropriate circumstances. Similarly in the case of "ringing the bell" and "calling people to dinner," the former does not cause the latter (though the former might be said to bear a "causal" relation to the action "making people gather for dinner"); rather, "calling people to dinner" is a redescription of "ringing the bell" warranted by the conventions of a particular community.

Alvin Goldman refers to the instrumental relation of action under one description to action under another as "level-generation," and gives a helpful typology of generating relations. See *A Theory of Human Action* (Englewood Cliffs, N.J.: Prentice-Hall, 1970), chap. 2. Lewis White Beck discusses the role of causal regularities and social conventions in providing rules for describing action in *The Actor and the Spectator* (New Haven: Yale University Press, 1975).

3. The issue between the mind-body dualist and his opponent concerns *where* to stop, not *whether* to stop, this regress. Both must appeal at some point to actions that are intentionally simple.

4. The terminology of "basic actions" was introduced by Arthur Danto in his article "What We Can Do," *The Journal of Philosophy,* 60 (1963):

435-45, and in "Basic Actions," *American Philosophical Quarterly,* 2 (1965): 141-48. He revised and reworked the concept in his book *Analytical Philosophy of Action* (Cambridge: Cambridge University Press, 1973). Others have since picked up the terminology of basic actions and developed it for their own purposes; see, for example, Goldman, *A Theory of Human Action,* chap. 3.

5. Given an instrumental action sequence, do we have one action and several descriptions or several distinct actions? This question has received a good deal of attention recently (see, for example, the articles by Goldman, Thompson, and Thalberg in *The Journal of Philosophy,* 68 [1971]). G. E. M. Anscombe was probably the first to raise the question explicitly (see her book *Intention,* 2d ed. [Ithaca, N.Y.: Cornell University Press, 1963], in which she suggests that an instrumental action sequence is best described as one action with several descriptions [p. 46]). Donald Davidson has also come to this conclusion (see his essay "Actions, Reasons, and Causes," in *The Philosophy of Action,* ed. A. R. White [Oxford: Oxford University Press, 1968]). A. I. Goldman convincingly criticizes these proposals and insists that in such cases we have several distinct actions (*A Theory of Human Action,* chap. 1). Neither position is entirely convincing. It seems odd to say, in the case we have been considering, that "pulling the rope" and "ringing the bell" are distinct actions. These intentional-action descriptions are logically distinct, and the performances they call attention to will often be distinct, but in this case they "go together," they coincide in one performance that can be described in both ways. In this case we might say that we have an intentionally complex action, an action that involves identifiable sub-acts. For the purposes of my discussion, however, it is not necessary to sort out all of the complex issues that surround the individuation of intentional actions and sub-actions.

6. "You have a donkey, so have I, and they graze in the same field. The day comes when I conceive a dislike for mine. I go to shoot it, draw a bead on it, fire: the brute falls in its tracks. I inspect the victim, and find to my horror it is *your* donkey. I appear on your doorstep with the remains and say—what? 'I say, old sport, I'm awfully sorry, etc., I've shot your donkey *by accident*'? Or *by mistake*'? Then again, I go to shoot my donkey as before, draw a bead on it, fire—but as I do so, the beasts move, and to my horror yours falls. Again the scene on the doorstep—what do I say? 'By mistake'? Or 'by accident'?" (J. L. Austin, "A Plea for Excuses," in *Essays in Philosophical Psychology,* ed. D. Gustafson [Garden City, N.Y.: Doubleday-Anchor, 1964], p. 10).

7. Cf. Jack W. Meiland's discussion of purposive and nonpurposive intentions in *The Nature of Intention* (London: Methuen & Co., 1970), chap. 1.

8. Gilbert Ryle, *The Concept of Mind* (New York: Barnes & Noble, 1949), chap. 2.

9. In addition to cases in which we disagree with an agent about *what* he intends in his action, there may also be cases in which we disagree with him about *whether* his behavior is intentional. We might insist that an agent did in fact have a purpose in behavior that he took to be unintentional action (e.g., a mistake or accident) or a subintentional automatism (e.g., a bodily reflex). We have just noted some of the complexities involved in making

judgments about whether an action is intentional or unintentional. We will comment later on the smooth transition from subintentional bodily processes to intentional action in the life of a bodily agent. This integration of levels of activity makes it difficult to know how to classify some human behaviors that occupy the boundary between the autonomic and the intentional. (See the discussion of the bodily basis of intentional action in Chap. 5, sec. 3 herein, especially pp. 95-96.)

10. On desires, beliefs, and intentions for future action "causing" behavior that is not intentional, see R. Chisholm's "Freedom and Action," in *Freedom and Determinism,* ed. K. Lehrer (New York: Random House, 1966), pp. 11-44.

11. We must note, in addition to reflex behaviors, one other important class of examples of unintentional performance of an intended action. Suppose that I plan to meet a friend at the library at 8:30 Wednesday morning. On the day that I take to be Tuesday, I show up at the library at 8:30 to get a book and there encounter my friend. It comes to light that I lost track of a day, and that it is in fact Wednesday, not Tuesday. I will then have performed the behavior that I intended, but I will not have done so intentionally. This example illustrates an earlier point about unintentional action—namely, that a performance of description A is not intentional if A is not a description of the project the agent was trying to carry through. In such a case the failure of my behavior to count as intentional action is due not to a lack of intentional control over my performance, but rather to the fact that the intention in accord with which I acted was not that of "meeting my friend at the library Wednesday morning at 8:30."

12. See Anscombe, *Intention,* sec. 22; Meiland, *Nature of Intention,* pp. 35-42; and H. A. Prichard, "Acting, Willing, Desiring," in *The Philosophy of Action*.

13. This does not entail, however, that one cannot predict one's future intentional actions. There are situations in which it makes sense to speak this way—for instance, when one is trying to imagine what one will do in remote or unlikely circumstances or when one is commenting upon his own character patterns (particularly one's weaknesses). In a psychological determinism it might make sense to speak of all intentional actions as predictable.

14. On the latter see Anscombe, *Intention,* pp. 89-90.

15. Anscombe, *Intention,* p. 6.

16. "Now it may be that a correct description of the role of intention in our actions will not be relevant to the question of free will; in any case I suspect that this was Wittgenstein's view; therefore in giving this antifreewill picture he was at liberty simply to leave the role of intention quite obscure" (Anscombe, *Intention,* p. 7).

17. "If a proposition describing event e is deducible from propositions expressing laws of nature and prior events $c_1, c_2, \ldots, c_k$ the events $c_1, c_2, \ldots, c_k$ will be said to *causally necessitate* event e" (Goldman, *Theory of Human Action,* p. 173). Goldman includes wants, or desires, among the events that causally necessitate action. This claim decisively distinguishes his position from the neurological determinism that I have sketched out here.

18. It might be argued that the relation between a brain event and its simultaneous epiphenomenon is not a causal relation. It is not necessary to

decide exactly how this relation should be conceived. The crucial point here is that the particular determinism we are considering is generated by insisting that relations of "causal necessitation" hold between successive sets of neurological events but do *not* hold either between successive psychological events or between psychological events and succeeding neurological events.

It is important to note that a rejection of this physical determinism is not necessarily a rejection of (a) every theory that proposes a correspondence of mental processes and brain processes, or (b) the possibility that a complete causal account might be given of the neurological events corresponding to mental processes. Some philosophers have argued that neurological processes and mental processes might be thought of as sets of exactly simultaneous events each necessary and sufficient for the occurrence of the other (see Goldman's discussion of "simultaneous nomic equivalents" in *A Theory of Human Action,* pp. 161-65). If brain events and mental processes are simultaneous nomic equivalents, then neither a particular neurological event nor the corresponding psychological event could be said to cause the other, since causality is a one-way relation of necessity and sufficiency (see Goldman, p. 161, n. 51); rather, both the neurological event and the corresponding psychological event have an equal status as cause of the next phase of neurological-psychological activity. This allows us to give a significant role to the agent's intention in explaining his behavior, for on this account the agent's intention (understood as a psychological event of desiring, or wanting) causes behavior that conforms to his intention. It appears, however, that this will leave us with a combined neurological-psychological determinism unless some "looseness" is built into the order of sequence of these complex events. This looseness might appear in neurological-psychological events that are underdetermined (i.e., that have necessary but not sufficient conditions). In that case we might speak of the agent as the uncaused cause of his action. Austin Farrer has some interesting speculations on these topics in *The Freedom of the Will,* 2d ed. (London: A. & C. Black, 1963), chaps. 2-4, and especially chap. 5.

The notion of "simultaneous nomic equivalents" is not unproblematic, and in any case shares the highly speculative character of all philosophical remarks on the relation of mind and brain that are not strictly remarks about the relations of concepts. There are some good reasons to think that a mind-brain identity theory or even a weaker mind-brain correlation theory does not provide an appropriate model for understanding the relation of our complex conscious operations and their neurological foundation. Kenneth Sayre, for example, insists that an "information processing" model is best able to handle the subtleties of human conscious activity, and that the "characteristics that govern the processing of this information insofar as it results in conscious response are not processes destined to yield explanation in physical terms" (*Consciousness: A Study in Minds and Machines* [New York: Random House, 1969], p. 212; see also chap. 8 passim).

19. On the conceivability of physical determinism, see Norman Malcolm's "Explaining Behavior," *The Philosophical Review,* 76 (1967) and "The Conceivability of Mechanism," *The Philosophical Review,* 77 (1968).

20. This discussion leaves open the question of whether in fact we are agents or merely complex organic mechanisms. One might argue that a

mechanistic conception of man cannot be true because it is incoherent or otherwise conceptually impossible. But I have argued a different point, namely, that a mechanistic conception of agency and intentional action is impossible; that is, I have argued that the concept of intentional action is incompatible with physical determinism. But it does not follow from this that physical determinism is false. *If* the physical determinist's theory describes a logically possible world, then we must argue about whether that theory describes *our* world. To point out that a concept of human agency is deeply rooted in our ordinary self-understanding does not rid us of the need to argue with the physical determinist, for the whole conceptual structure that makes possible talk of intentional action might be displaced by the physical determinist's explanatory structure. Richard Bernstein, drawing upon Wilfred Sellars, put this point nicely: "It may be that everything that the conceptual analyst wants to maintain about the distinctive and nonreducible nature of the language of action is true for the way in which man normally conceives of himself. Yet nevertheless, it is theoretically possible to question the entire 'manifest' framework, to argue *not* that such a conceptual framework can be *reduced*, but that it can be *replaced*. We may have good reasons for saying that even though the conceptual framework or language of action is nonreducible, it can be replaced by a better scientific (and even mechanistic) framework" (*Praxis and Action* [Philadelphia: University of Pennsylvania Press, 1971], p. 259).

The point is an important one if, as Bernstein argues, analytic philosophers of action have tended to assume too easily that in laying bare the structure of our ordinary ways of thinking about ourselves we lay bare the structure of reality. Clarifying conceptual structures does not settle metaphysical questions, though it does help us accurately locate the points at which there is significant opposition between conceptual frameworks. And this may turn out to be all the metaphysics we can do.

21. Sophisticated versions of this psychological determinism have been worked out by a number of authors. In particular, see Davidson's "Actions, Reasons, and Causes" and Goldman's *Theory of Human Action.* A theory of this type requires that intentions be understood as a species of desires, or wants, and that these desires be treated as conscious events that cause action. Contemporary philosophical psychology has displayed a remarkable unanimity in resisting these views, and much of Davidson's article and Goldman's book are devoted to answering well-known objections. For standard arguments against the view that an agent's reasons for action cause him to act as he does, see Ryle's *Concept of Mind;* Anscombe's *Intention;* R. S. Peters's *The Concept of Motivation* (London: Routledge & Kegan Paul, 1960); Melden's *Free Action;* Anthony Kenny's *Action, Emotion, and Will* (New York: Humanities Press, 1963); Charles Taylor's *The Explanation of Behavior* (London: Routledge & Kegan Paul, 1964); and Richard Taylor's *Action and Purpose* (Englewood Cliffs, N.J.: Prentice-Hall, 1966; New York: Humanities Press, 1973).

CHAPTER 3

1. Rene Descartes, *Meditations on First Philosophy,* in *Descartes: Philo-*

sophical Writings, trans. G. E. M. Anscombe and Peter Geach (Edinburgh: Nelson, 1954), pp. 114-15.

2. Letter from Princess Elizabeth to Descartes, 6-16 May 1643, in *Descartes: Philosophical Writings,* p. 274.

3. Letter from Descartes to Princess Elizabeth, 28 June 1643, in *Descartes: Philosophical Writings,* p. 281.

4. From the "Synopsis of the Six Following Meditations" that Descartes placed at the beginning of his *Meditations on First Philosophy,* in *The Philosophical Works of Descartes,* trans. Elizabeth Haldane and G. R. T. Ross (Cambridge: Cambridge University Press, 1973), pp. 140-43.

5. Letter from Descartes to Princess Elizabeth, 28 June 1643, in *Descartes: Philosophical Writings,* p. 281.

6. For a rehearsal of the argument, see Gilbert Ryle's *The Concept of the Mind* (New York: Barnes & Noble, 1949), p. 67. A. I. Melden develops a similar argument in *Free Action* (London: Routledge & Kegan Paul, 1961), pp. 53-55.

7. Letter of Descartes to More, 15 April 1649, in *Descartes: Philosophical Letters,* trans. Anthony Kenny (Oxford: Clarendon Press, 1970), p. 252.

8. In the Introduction to this text I note that Gordon Kaufman's account of God's transcendence and self-revelation may be indebted to just this way of exploiting mind-body dualism; I will return to these issues later in this chapter.

9. For the sake of verbal simplicity, I will refer to the complex set of descriptions that give the concept of mind its content as the family of "mental predicates." This label is philosophically inept, but is less awkward than the more accurate alternatives (e.g., "mind-making characteristics").

10. Ryle, *Concept of Mind,* pp. 15-23.

11. Ibid., p. 16.

12. See Stuart Hampshire's *Thought and Action* (London: Chatto & Windus, 1959), chap. 1.

13. I will return to the subject of these strategies in Chap. 4, pp. 77ff.

14. Cf. Austin Farrer's claim that "the causal joint (so to speak) between infinite and finite action plays and in the nature of the case can play no part in our concern with God and his will" (*Faith and Speculation* [New York: New York University Press, 1967], p. 65; see also chaps. 4-5 therein).

15. Gordon Kaufman, *God the Problem* (Cambridge: Harvard University Press, 1972), pp. 63-64.

16. See, for instance, F. Michael McLain, "On Theological Models," *Harvard Theological Review,* 62 (1969): 155-87.

17. In his review of *God the Problem,* David Kelsey points out that Kaufman's analysis of the self provides essential backing for his claim that the *concept* of God as a personal agent is "appropriate" to the transcendent divine *reality* ("Can God Be Agent Without Body?", *Interpretation,* 27 [1973]:358-62). More generally, Kaufman's quasi-dualist account of persons provides him with a familiar instance in which we encounter a cognitive limit and yet can also properly speak of an active reality *beyond* that limit.

> "On this model God cannot be identified with what is accessible to or within our experience: rather this Limit must be grasped as the medium through which God encounters us (as noises and gestures are

the media for finite selves), God himself being conceived as the dynamic acting reality beyond the Limit" (*God the Problem,* pp. 64-65).

If Kaufman must give up the understanding of persons upon which this proposal is based, then one of the fundamental structures of his theological program seems to collapse.

CHAPTER 4

1. P. F. Strawson, "Persons," in *Individuals: An Essay in Descriptive Metaphysics* (Garden City: Doubleday-Anchor, 1963), pp. 81-113.

2. Ibid., pp. 97-98. Note that this definition of the concept "person" creates a logical class that includes a broader range of subjects than we ordinarily associate with the word: not only are human beings persons, but so are sentient organisms of all kinds.

3. Ibid., pp. 100-101.

4. Ibid., p. 101.

5. Ibid., p. 98.

6. Ibid., p. 96.

7. Alvin Plantinga calls it the "predication principle" (in *God and Other Minds* [Ithaca, N.Y.: Cornell University Press, 1967], p. 230).

8. Strawson, pp. 94-95, n. 3.

9. It is important to note that the predication rule (viz., that a predicate can have a first-person use only if it also has a third-person use) will follow from Strawson's claim about the idea of a predicate (i.e., that it must be logically possible to ascribe a predicate to more than one individual) only if "individual" is taken to mean *distinct entity* (e.g., a person) rather than *instance* (e.g., either a person or an event involving a person). It seems quite reasonable to say that the idea of a predicate is correlative with a range of distinguishable instances in which it is logically possible to ascribe the predicate, but this is a weaker claim than Strawson is making, for in this case a predicate could be restricted in its use to just one individual (e.g., a person) but be used in multiple instances (e.g., various episodes involving that person). A solipsist might then grant that there are many instances in which a state of consciousness is ascribable, though all of those instances will be first-person ascriptions. This would satisfy the required logic of predication, but it would not yield the predication rule Strawson needs for his argument against the dualist.

The predication rule, then, does not follow from the very idea of a predicate unless an argument can be made for the stronger claim about the logic of predication, namely, that the idea of a predicate is correlative with a range of distinguishable individuals *qua* entities to whom the predicate can be ascribed. One very important way of arguing for this stronger claim is to assert the impossibility of a "private language," a language necessarily restricted to first-person use. It is possible to argue that the necessary conditions for the formation and use of a sign system cannot be met if there is only one user. Although Strawson does not construct or even mention private-language arguments, a full defense of this first premise would involve appeal to an argument that has this force.

10. Strawson, pp. 96-97.

11. It is fair to ask, for example, whether the particular sense in which the dualist is committed to treating first-person ascription of states of consciousness as a necessary condition for third-person ascription does in fact clash with the predication rule. The predication rule requires only that if a predicate is to be self-ascribed by a speaker of the language, it must be *logically possible* to ascribe that predicate to others. A predicate cannot be restricted in principle to first-person use. But does the dualist's use of first-person observations to provide an identifying relation for third-person use violate this rule?

The dualist cannot avoid giving first-person use a crucial role in securing the possibility of third-person ascription of states of consciousness, but he can refuse to say that in learning to ascribe states of consciousness one first acquires the capacity to refer to one's own states of consciousness and then develops the criteria needed to ascribe states of consciousness to others, since this would be outrageously artificial. The dualist may grant that we *learn* first- and third-person uses together, yet insist that his analogical argument provides the best (and, in his own scheme of thought, the only) structure of *justification* for third-person ascription. Taken this way, his account of third-person ascription of states of consciousness grants first-person use an epistemological priority but denies it logical independence. This, however, seems to be perfectly compatible with the predication rule. The predication rule makes third-person ascription of a predicate the "necessary condition" of first-person use in the sense that third-person ascription must be logically possible if there is to be any ascription whatsoever of that predicate. The dualist's analogical argument makes first-person use the "necessary condition" of third-person ascription in the sense that first-person use justifies the criteria we employ in third-person ascription. No logical circle is generated if these two senses of "necessary condition" are distinguished.

Alvin Plantinga offers a similar though more elegant criticism of Strawson in his book *God and Other Minds,* pp. 205-11, 227-32.

12. Strawson, p. 96.

13. Strawson's account of the basic structure of our references is not beyond challenge. See, for example, Bernard Williams's *Problems of Self* (Cambridge: Cambridge University Press, 1973), chap. 7. Rather than argue out the merits of Strawson's claims, however, I will contend that even within the terms of his discussion it is possible to identify God as a unique subject of speech.

14. Strawson, p. 5.

15. Ibid.

16. In his discussion of problems associated with the identification of God's actions, Robert King struggles briefly with the implications of story-relative identification (*The Meaning of God* [Philadelphia: Fortress Press, 1973], pp. 124-26). His difficulties arise, at least in part, because he works with only two of the modes of identification that Strawson introduces: story-relative and demonstrative identification. Given these alternatives, King opts for the former. He recognizes, however, that this will not satisfy the theist who wants to make "a claim of fact." He therefore adds the

proviso that the Christian story "is interpretive of what is going on in the world" (p. 125). King does not develop this point about the interpretive relevance of the Christian story. But it is clear that if Christian talk about God is to connect with "the larger world of events in which we all participate" (p. 125), then reference to God cannot be strictly story-relative. King acknowledges this, but does not know how to escape the unacceptable alternatives he borrowed from Strawson. "For now the important thing to realize is that the story has empirical relevance. . . . This may not constitute demonstrative identification of the sort that Strawson thinks is important, but at least it means that the identification is something other than merely story-relative" (p. 126).

It is my contention that there are several ways in which God can be identified that are neither simply demonstrative nor purely story-relative. All of these depend upon certain accompanying suppositions (the elements of a theistic story) that support the reference to God. But since the theistic story is carefully connected with our shared world of objects and events, reference to God is not story-relative (i.e., referentially isolated). I hold that such references are story-bound rather than story-relative.

17. Strawson, pp. 14ff.

18. Ibid., pp. 81-100.

19. There may be reasons not to speak of events as particulars. Events, perhaps, might be analyzed into relations between particulars (*qua* entities), though I have argued that an intentional action cannot be analyzed strictly in these terms. In any case, events are identifiable either as particulars themselves or as relations of particulars.

20. Cf. W. D. Hudson's *A Philosophical Approach to Religion* (London: Macmillan, 1974), pp. 165-76, in which Hudson suggests that "spatio-temporal events may serve as a substitute for a physical body in the case of God" (p. 173). He goes on to explain that we may identify a being who is not located in space by identifying certain spatio-temporal events as his actions. In defending this suggestion Hudson makes the disconcerting remark that there is "some kind of Cartesian parallelism in the last analysis between mind and body even in the case of human agents" (p. 174). His argument, however, does not depend upon this claim. As he develops his case he seems to be arguing that (1) the identification of spatio-temporal events may be a necessary (though not sufficient) condition for the identification of an action, but (2) the identification of a physical body (or of a determinate location in space) is neither a necessary nor a sufficient condition for the identification of an agent.

21. This, of course, is the question that Langdon Gilkey raised in so pointed a way about biblical theology. Kaufman and Ogden both respond to Gilkey's question by offering an account, as Gilkey puts it, of "what we might mean in systematic theology by the general activity of God" ("Cosmology, Ontology, and the Travail of Biblical Language," *Journal of Religion,* 41 [1961]: 204). Kaufman and Ogden deemphasize the notion of special acts of God in history and center their proposals upon God's relation to nature and human history as a whole. One of the results of this theological strategy is that we are left without any simple foundation for the identification of God as an agent of intentional actions. Kaufman and Ogden allow that specific events can be called divine actions in the sense that these events

particularly exemplify for us the character and direction of God's universal activity in history. But properly speaking, God's activity lies at the foundation of natural and historical processes and cannot be identified as a distinct event or series of events within those processes. This means that the identification of God's activity is dependent upon the adoption of a general account of God's relation to the world.

Providing a general account of this sort *is* an important part of the task facing any theologian who would talk of divine action. "Unless we have some conception of how God acts in ordinary events," Gilkey contends, "we can hardly know what our analogical words mean when we say: 'He acts uniquely in this event' " (pp. 204-205). I intend to argue a similar point: a theologian can identify events as God's actions only within the context provided by a wider theistic "story" about our world. But it is important to notice that Kaufman and Ogden offer accounts of the "general activity of God" that take it for granted that God cannot or does not act in a special way in particular events within the world. Kaufman expresses this in especially strong terms: "Our experience is of a unified and orderly world; in such a world acts of God (in the traditional sense) are not merely improbable or difficult to believe: they are literally inconceivable" (*God the Problem* [Cambridge: Harvard University Press, 1972], pp. 134-35). It is not obvious that Kaufman is right on either conceptual or contemporary cultural grounds, though I will not launch a full-fledged discussion of these questions here. We might note in passing that if Kaufman is right, then his own proposal may be in trouble. As we have already seen, Kaufman suggests that we think of history in its entirety as God's "master act." But this alone does not spare us the difficulties associated with talk of particular divine actions in history, for it is incoherent to speak of a master act (i.e., a long-term intention) without any sub-acts that enact it. If Kaufman is to avoid saying that God is at work (however subtly) in the actual events of nature and human history, then we must locate all of God's activity "at the beginning" of the world process, as an action of laying down its structure or laws of development. "It is God's master act that gives the world the structure it has and gives natural and historical processes their direction. Speaking of God's act in this sense in no way threatens the unity and order of the world as a whole" (p. 138). This, however, leaves him with a position strikingly parallel to that of eighteenth-century deism. The implications of Kaufman's proposals for other doctrinal questions (e.g., in Christology) are worth pondering.

22. Some very difficult and long-standing problems arise here. Perhaps the most notable set of issues clusters around traditional disputes over divine grace and human freedom. How is God's activity in forming and influencing human lives woven around human self-determination? Can both the sovereignty of God's intention and the independence of the human will be maintained? This may finally be a more telling question than that of whether talk of divine action is any longer meaningful for us "modern men," though the latter has dominated recent discussions of divine action.

In this connection it may be fruitful to develop a nondualistic "interpersonal model" not simply for the transcendence of God but also for his active relatedness to creatures. The relation of God and human beings can probably be better understood if our dominant analogy is the formation of a relationship between persons rather than the discrete "act of will" that can be neatly ascribed to one agent or another. We may, that is, avoid some of the sharp oppositions of past discussions if we subordinate concepts of free choice, powers of action, and responsibility to an understanding of the more subtle dynamics at work in the formation of relationships of friendship, trust, or love. In this regard see Austin Farrer, *Faith and Speculation* (New York: New York University Press, 1967), especially chaps. 3 and 4, and J. R. Lucas, *Freedom and Grace* (Grand Rapids: Wm. B. Eerdmans, 1976).

23. It is important to note that in speaking of a religious "story" I am using the term in an extended sense to refer *not only* to biblical narrative, but also to the conceptually refined theological "story" that is developed out of the narrative. One might say, for example, that Whiteheadian metaphysics has received theological attention because the story it tells about the world promises to be helpful in developing a theological story about God.

24. It might be better to say that "taken together they represent a possible form of experience," for our story about agents and intentional action is not so much *brought to* our experience of persons as it is *constitutive of* it. A similar point can be made about the theistic story when it profoundly grasps the imagination and comes to inform experience pervasively.

25. Austin Farrer's *Finite and Infinite,* 2d ed. (London: A. & C. Black, Dacre Press, 1959), is a sustained effort to unpack the suppositions about man and the world involved in the theistic idea of a relation of radical ontological dependence.

26. One might want to add "or produced in me directly (i.e., other than by producing a desire or intention to perform that action)."

27. Note that here the possibility arises of an anti-dualist argument based upon the limitations of the act-agent connection as an individuating relation. The dualist must say that every bodily action has an instrumental substructure (i.e., no bodily action is a basic action). But this means that the dualist cannot uniquely identify an agent on the basis of any bodily action, since bodily actions could always be simultaneously ascribed to more than one mental agent. Hence, it appears that the dualist could never individuate mental agents at all. Only if bodily actions can be basic actions will it be possible to identify agents uniquely on the basis of their bodily actions, for only in this case can we reliably say that for a particular bodily action there can be just one agent. An agent whose basic actions include bodily actions will, of course, be a psychophysical unit.

The dualist can always insist that for any body there is just one mental agent. He might even offer an analogical argument as a way of defending this "one body, one agent" principle: "I know from my own case that bodily action is brought about by a single agent, hence I infer that the bodily actions of others are to be ascribed to just one agent." This agential form of the analogical argument, however, would face the same objections as the traditional form. The dualist would, in effect, be asking us to approve his story about persons (i.e., that we are mental agents who are uniquely associated with a single body), but in the face of an arguably less problematic alternative (i.e., of treating some bodily actions as basic actions, and therefore of treating bodily agents as psychophysical units), the dualist's story could be reasonably set aside.

CHAPTER 5

1. The danger in this procedure is that it might entail begging certain questions. The advantages, however, are twofold. First, we are not sidetracked into a lengthy discussion of elusive issues that do not contribute directly to our main concerns. Second, our discussion will be only loosely connected to any particular answer that might be given to these theoretical questions, and so will be both less closely tied to their inevitable weaknesses and better able to survive the revision or abandonment they may suffer.

2. It is precisely the task of medicine to find the *means* by which we can modify (in intentionally complex actions) the subintentional processes at work in bodily life.

3. If the development of a new basic action were itself a basic action, it would be impossible to make sense of the statement that at an earlier time the agent was not capable of that action. We can intentionally expand the scope of our basic actions only by employing some *means* of doing so, though that means will most likely involve a program of disciplined, gradual extension of existing capacities for action, as when we undertake a program of strength-building exercises.

4. Austin Farrer offers an apt metaphor here: he suggests that intentional action must develop as an "embroidery" along the borders of bodily life (*Finite and Infinite*, 2d ed. [London: A. & C. Black, Dacre Press, 1959], pp. 178, 229).

5. In two of his books Austin Farrer offers some penetrating observations on how an agent's interest is captured, focused, criticized, and refined. See *Finite and Infinite*, chap. 12 and *The Freedom of the Will*, 2d ed. (London: A. & C. Black, 1963), chap. 11.

6. Austin Farrer offers a detailed and illuminating account of "the bodily bias" of our intentional activity (see *Finite and Infinite*, chap. 15).

7. The term *personal identity* bears a number of interrelated meanings both in ordinary usage and in philosophical discussion. In speaking of personal identity we are sometimes pointing to that network of characteristic interests, attitudes, values, character traits, and so on that make an individual a distinctive personality. The phrase is also used as part of the vocabulary for stating philosophical quandaries about the persistence of a person as a single individual throughout the dramatic changes that take place across the span of his life. This might be termed a problem about the identity-through-time of persons.

My concern in this section is with personal identity in the first of these senses, although a discussion of personal identity in this sense inevitably raises questions about personal identity in the second sense. In describing the complex patterns of action in which an agent's personal identity (in the first sense) appears, we suppose that a diverse array of actions performed at different times can be ascribed to a single individual. While I will not take up all of the questions raised by this "singleness" of the subject of character descriptions, the remarks I make about persons as distinctive individuals will be relevant to this underlying set of questions. Part of any consideration of the identity-through-time of persons must be a discussion of personal identity in the sense in which I will be using that phrase.

8. Continuities of project and continuities of character will coincide, of

course, when an agent makes it his project to undertake actions that are subject to a particular evaluation (e.g., if he tries to be morally good).

9. G. E. M. Anscombe suggests a distinction between intention and motive (*Intention,* 2d ed. [Ithaca, N.Y.: Cornell University Press, 1963], sec. 12), or otherwise expressed, between intentions as "forward-looking motives" and motives proper, that is, "backward-looking motives" and "motives-in-general" (secs. 13-14). My point is parallel to hers. We concern ourselves not only with what an agent intends but also with the factors that help us understand why he intends what he intends, where the answer to the question "Why?" does not involve citing a further intention at work in his action.

Austin Farrer offers a lengthy discussion of the "concentration of the background" of action in each of an agent's projects (*Finite and Infinite*, chaps. 17 and 18). The background Farrer has in mind is "memory in the widest possible sense of that term" (p. 199). He indicates that this includes "not only contents of past experiences, but also habits and formed desires and previous resolutions and tendencies of action" (p. 200). Much of what I say below is informed by Farrer's quite subtle analysis of the ongoing role played by our past experience in our present actions.

10. Robert King, *The Meaning of God* (Philadelphia: Fortress Press, 1973), p. 65. King goes on to argue that this failure of the intention-action model has important implications for theology: "Since it is generally supposed that the word 'God' names an enduring Subject, and not simply an ongoing process, it may be necessary to supplement the model of personal agency with that of the elusive 'I'" (p. 65). If an account of persons as agents finally cannot do justice to the enduring human (or divine) subject, then we must turn elsewhere. King's proposed remedy, the model of the elusive "I," is itself a bit elusive, however. When King introduces this idea he appeals to the immediate consciousness of possessing a unique perspective on the world (pp. 21ff.). The owner of this perspective does not appear directly as an item in experience; rather, the owner is the subject of experience who is continuously present as the condition for there being a unified experiential perspective at all. It is hard to know just what to say about this transcendental subject. "In the last analysis, it may be that all that can be said of the elusive self is simply that it is. . . . For it is indicative of a persistent subject of action and therefore irreducible source of action" (p. 65). Perhaps we could take this elusive "I" as a kind of cipher or pseudonym for the complex unity that constitutes us as selves, and refuse to treat it as naming an entity. But by placing the notion of an "enduring Subject" in juxtaposition to that of an "ongoing process," King at least suggests that we understand this elusive subject as a persisting entity whose self-identity underlies the continuous activity of the agent's life. But if this is what elusive subjectivity means, then it is not clear that this notion is intelligible at all, much less that it is able to supplement in an illuminating way our understanding of persons as agents. King turns to this notion, as he explains in the passage above, because he fears that the intention-action model cannot do justice to the bearer of an identity that persists from action to action. It cannot be denied that there are puzzles to struggle with in trying to grasp and represent the unity of an agent's life. But King never explains why he thinks that an understanding of persons as agents fails to account for "an identity which persists beyond a

particular action." The bulk of this chapter represents an argument against this claim. If we assume that "self," or "subject," must mean self-identical substance, then of course talk of the self as a unity of activity will not be satisfying. But that supposition begs the question. We may understand the identity-through-time of the agent in terms of the continuity and integration of the activity that constitutes his life. But in this case we cannot set the idea of an enduring subject in opposition to that of an ongoing process.

11. This way of thinking about persons owes a great deal to Austin Farrer's work in *Finite and Infinite*. While I have not followed him on matters of detail in action theory, my discussion in this chapter is indebted to the fundamental strategies at work in his description of the human agent. At the heart of Farrer's project is an attempt to understand the "real connection" that binds constituents together in an irreducible (i.e., substantial) unit. Since the person as a whole provides the paradigm of substantial unity for Farrer, he is committed to understanding bodily life and intentional action as constituents in a single integrated structure. He describes the agent as a hierarchically organized system of activity. The unity of this operative system, Farrer argues, cannot be located in "a transcendent unit, the self in itself, the pure subject" (p. 221); rather, we must describe the many unities (of bodily life, of memory, and of action and character) that appear in the ongoing activity of being a self, and we must point to their interdependence. This procedure does not deliver into our hands *the* unity of the self, however. Farrer seems to say that the complex unity of an individual life can be intuited but not described. If Farrer is right, then there *is* an elusiveness about the unity of the self, but it is not the elusiveness of an unchanging substance that somehow persists beneath the ongoing process of the agent's life; rather, it is the elusiveness of a unity that we try to understand by making distinctions. The unity we live, Farrer suggests, can never be captured in the net of philosophical analysis. "It cannot be too often said that the function of the intellect is always to mark significant distinctions. . . . We may grasp the elements of a pattern one by one, and even see, by a constructional synthesis, how they supplement one another and are ordered towards a unity. But it is another thing to be aware of that unity in its unitary character, to intuit the unum" (p. 220). He goes on to say that "the unity of the self and its structural complication cannot be grasped in one; yet they imply and support one another" (p. 229).

CHAPTER 6

1. See Austin Farrer's *Finite and Infinite*, 2d ed. (London: A. & C. Black, Dacre Press, 1959), pp. 292-93, and *Faith and Speculation* (New York: New York University Press, 1967), chaps. 7 and 9.

2. We have immediate, or direct, intentional control over those segments of our activity that we can modify in basic actions. We are, of course, capable of indirectly modifying the human organism in intentionally complex actions. I have already suggested that it is the task of medicine to extend our knowledge of the means by which we can successfully intervene in bodily processes outside the range of our direct control.

3. In the discussion that follows (in this chapter and the next), I will

consider three possibilities:

(1) We might assert that God is embodied in both respects.
(2) We might assert that God is embodied in the first respect but deny that he is embodied in the second.
(3) We might deny that God is embodied in either respect.

The first two possibilities suggest variations on the proposal that God is embodied in the world. The third possibility will generate a somewhat more traditional theism. A fourth possibility—that God is embodied in the second respect but not in the first—is not very promising. The life of such an agent would be grounded in a given pattern of subintentional activity, but this given pattern would not take the form of organic life. This shares most of the difficulties of the first two proposals without sharing their distinctive strengths. But while it may be difficult to make use of this formal possibility in the doctrine of God, it might be quite helpful if we ever find ourselves ready once again to give angels a place in our theology!

4. The phrase "theologically adequate" does *not* denote an unproblematic shared criterion; rather, it states a *topic for debate* in the evaluation of theological proposals.

5. This move has been made by a number of theologians whose roots lie (at least in part) in the philosophy of Alfred North Whitehead. Charles Hartshorne is among the best known of these—see his books *Man's Vision of God* (New York: Harper & Row, 1941) and *The Divine Relativity* (New Haven: Yale University Press, 1948). See also Schubert Ogden's *The Reality of God* (New York: Harper & Row, 1963) and James McClendon's "Can There Be Talk about God-and-the-World?" *Harvard Theological Review,* 62 (1969): 33-49.

6. It is important to note at the outset that the proposal to think of God and the world as constituting a psychophysical unity, in the sense I have given that term, will differ from some process theologies in important respects. This is because the understanding of the bodily agent at work in Whiteheadian metaphysics is significantly different from that which I developed in the previous chapter.

If we take John Cobb as our example of a theologian's reading of Whitehead (since Hartshorne tends to be less closely tied to Whitehead's own metaphysical scheme), these differences become apparent. The person, Cobb says, is to be identified with the soul (*A Christian Natural Theology* [Philadelphia: Westminster Press, 1965], pp. 65-66). Without venturing into the details of Cobb's interpretation of Whitehead, there are two key points that we can note about the soul. First, the soul is an ontological unit in its own right, distinct from the body. At any moment the soul is always a single actual occasion of experience that is peculiarly dominant within the network of actual occasions (the "corpuscular society") that constitutes the body. The serially ordered society of these dominant actual occasions constitutes an "enduring object," an ongoing individual. This distinct enduring object bears a uniquely personal identity that is in some degree continuous through time. Hence Cobb can say, "It is the soul that is truly personal, the true subject. The body is the immediate environment of the person" (p. 66).

We must not stop simply with this distinctness of the soul, however, for the soul is a society of actual occasions, and every actual occasion is essentially relational, or social. Hence, a second point: the actual occasions that constitute the soul are themselves crucially constituted by their relations to the body (or, properly speaking, to the actual occasions that constitute the body). In its internal constitution the soul bears a unique reference to the body even though soul and body are ontologically distinct. This is one of the points at which a Whiteheadian account of the soul is distinguished from Cartesian dualism. A human soul is what it is by virtue of its relations to the body. Mind and body do not represent primitive metaphysical categories that can be defined independently of each other. Those aspects of reality that go by the names "mind" and "body" are understood in terms of a common categorical scheme that does not allow for a dichotomy between them. Nonetheless, the identification of the human soul with a particular enduring object within the psychophysical complex does lead to some peculiar results. On this view, for example, it is necessary to ask where in the brain the soul might be located and how it exercises its dominant influence over the actual occasions that constitute brain cells (see Cobb, pp. 82ff.).

Clearly, an appreciation of this scheme is crucial in understanding how a Whiteheadian would develop the suggestion that the world is God's body. In any theology grounded directly in Whiteheadian metaphysics, God will be a real individual in his own right, distinct from, though intimately related to, the real individuals who constitute the world process. In systematic language, God will be a single unperishing actual entity, or (as Cobb suggests) a distinctive society of serially ordered actual entities—that is to say, a temporally extended individual (see Cobb, pp. 185-92). The conditions for being an actual entity at all require that God be internally related to other actual entities, but God's life is distinct from theirs and achieves a unity and satisfaction that is uniquely his own.

There are some significant differences between these Whiteheadian patterns of thought and the proposals that I have been developing. As I have described the bodily agent, it is the psychophysical complex taken as an irreducible unit. An analysis of the psychophysical unit into subordinate structures does not yield an agent-plus-a-body, but rather yields simply the various constituents of the psychophysical complex that form an agent only as a whole. The agent is not a discrete entity that is uniquely related to a particular body; rather, the agent is the operative unity of bodily and intentional activity taken as a single complex individual. If God is understood as a psychophysical unit on this model, then the divine agent cannot be set in contrast to the world as an individual distinct from it. There can be no conjunction "God-and-the-world"; rather, there is a divine agent whose bodily life is the life of the universe. Among the family of process theologies, Hartshorne's proposals (particularly in his early work) come closest to this view.

In exploring the suggestion that the world be thought of as God's body, I work from the account of psychophysical agency I developed in Chapter 5 rather than from a Whiteheadian account of persons as embodied souls. Some of the criticisms that I level against the theology of cosmic organism might be avoided or more readily answered by a Whiteheadian development of the mind-body analogy, but the Whiteheadian scheme brings with it both some important difficulties of its own and a cumbersome technical argot.

7. Austin Farrer offers some significant objections to this picture of the universe as a single complex individual. See *Faith and Speculation*, chap. 10.

8. On the "ghost in the machine," see Gilbert Ryle's *The Concept of Mind* (New York: Barnes & Noble, 1949), pp. 15-16. On the "ghost in the universe," see McClendon's "Can There be Talk about God-and-the-World?" McClendon suggests that process theology and Ryle's philosophical psychology are natural allies. I think this may be true of Hartshorne's process theology, but it clearly is not true of any process theology that operates within Whitehead's metaphysical scheme. As we have noted, Whitehead understands the relation of mind and body as a relation of discrete (though internally related) entities. Hartshorne, on the other hand, tends to treat mind as the operative unity of the many bodily parts: "The body as a whole, as a dynamic individual unit (not a collection) or—it is the same thing—as a mind, wills: the parts of the body (which may be minds, but not *that* mind) respond" (*Man's Vision of God*, p. 182). If we disregard Hartshorne's panpsychism, his contention does bear some affinity to Ryle's insistence that mind is not a distinct substance but rather a quality of the person (the psychophysical unit) as a whole.

9. Hartshorne stresses the importance of combining self-body and self-self (interpersonal) patterns of relation in talking of God's relation to the world (see *Man's Vision of God*, chap. 5). The need to join the latter to the former is clear. The possibility of carrying off this fusion in a convincing way is less so, as we shall see.

10. Hartshorne, *Man's Vision of God*, chap. 5.

11. You will recall my suggestion in Chapter 4 that a single basic action cannot be ascribed to more than one agent (p. 161).

Hartshorne takes the "immediacy" of the knowledge I have of my bodily states and the "directness" of the control I have of my bodily actions as one of the key marks of the relation of mind to body (*Man's Vision of God*, pp. 178-80). If mind-body and interpersonal relations are to be combined, it must be possible for interpersonal relations to be immediate (p. 188). Hence, we find Hartshorne speaking of an "immediate sharing of feeling" with the cells of my body, taken as primitive sub-centers of experience (pp. 188ff., 289ff.; see also Hartshorne's insistence in *The Divine Relativity*, p. 91, that God "literally contains" all experiences in the universe). It is not clear what he has in mind here. He seems to be suggesting that a cell's experience simultaneously appears as a constituent in my experience. This is not only to say that the cell and I have qualitatively identical experiences, but also that the occurrence of the cell's experience is the occurrence of my experience. But in this case we may wonder whether there are two subjects of experience. Hartshorne may refuse to take experiential distinctness as one of the criteria of subjective identity, but then how are individual subjects to be distinguished?

This is another point at which Hartshorne's discussion of God's relation to the world, while drawing its inspiration from Whitehead, differs from Whitehead significantly. We have already noted that Whitehead does not treat the relation of body and mind as a relation of parts to a whole, but rather as the relation of a distinct actual occasion (or personally ordered series of actual occasions) to a complex society of other actual occasions. We should also note that Whitehead does not allow for any sharing of subjectivity between actual occasions. The "conformance" of one occasion's subjective form of feeling to that of another plays an important role in Whitehead's metaphysic, but that which the feeling conforms to is the other's subjective form of feeling in its settled determinacy (its "objective immortality"). No actual entity, including God, experiences the subjective becoming (the inner process of concrescence) of another actual entity.

On social imminence and transcendence in Whitehead, see William Christian's lucid study *An Interpretation of Whitehead's Metaphysics* (New Haven: Yale University Press, 1951), chaps. 3, 6-9; note also Christian's discussion of the relation of Hartshorne's proposals to Whitehead's metaphysical scheme in chap. 19, pp. 403-409.

12. William Austin offers a clear and careful account of the use of complementary models in theology; see his *Waves, Particles, and Paradox*, Rice University Studies, vol. 53, no. 2 (Houston: William Marsh Rice University, 1967).

13. Farrer, *Faith and Speculation*, p. 158.

14. Would Hartshorne affirm the embodiment of God in *this* sense? I think it is clear that he would not, though the issue is complex. The self-creativity of Hartshorne's God *is* limited in significant ways. But these limitations are not contingent limitations of the sort that characterize the activity of creatures (e.g., the particular limitations inherent in being a human agent); rather, they are necessary restrictions that reflect the founding principles of Hartshorne's metaphysical scheme. For Hartshorne, God's essence consists in being the supremely relative (and all-inclusive) self at the center of a world of subordinate selves. Because these subordinate selves have at least some capacity to determine the content of their own lives, God's possibilities are limited by the decisions of others. God cannot be without a social world; nor can he make of the world whatever he will: he is preeminently influential in shaping the direction of the world process, and so is as profoundly self-creative as any agent can be (given the terms of Hartshorne's metaphysical scheme), but his freedom does not extend to determining whether he will be related to others in a network of unfolding social relations. The ultimate principles of metaphysical analysis are those that define creative becoming as a social process; God's creative activity is explained in terms of these principles rather than vice versa.

15. I noted in Chapter 2 that the concepts of intentional action and freedom of action are separable, so that it is possible to speak of actions that are intentional but not free. Provisionally we can say that an intentional action would be "determined" if its motivational background constitutes a set of causally sufficient conditions for undertaking that action and if all of the elements composing that background are themselves the outcome of causally sufficient events. It is not necessary, however, to thrash through all of the issues raised by this definition of "determinism" and the complementary definition of "freedom." It is enough here to acknowledge that the theologian is concerned to ascribe freedom to God in any relevant sense that can be given to that term. This does not settle any of the difficult questions that arise about the meaning or meaninglessness, compatibility or incompatibility of claims about freedom and determinism; it only acknowledges the theologian's special angle of interest in such discussions.

16. It is worth noting that there may be an important philosophical motive at work here as well. One may be convinced, following Whitehead, that internal relation to other subjects is a necessary condition for being a subject at all. Expressed in the language of agency, one might argue that interaction with other agents is a necessary condition for being an agent. If one accepts a principle of this sort, then relation to others will be an essential property of God. This might lead us to say that God's life as an agent consists of his activity of creating and sustaining creaturely agents. This would not, however, commit us to saying that the world is God's body, for the creature's life need not be a part of God's life, even though God's life consists in his creative engagement with creatures.

Furthermore, we should note the possibility of granting that relatedness is an essential structure of God's life and yet arguing that God's life is complete apart from his relation to his creatures, since the relatedness that is an essential property of God might not be his relatedness to creatures. We might argue that God's life includes an inherent differentiation and relatedness. It is obvious that such thinking has an important place in historic Christianity (i.e., in reflecting upon the Trinity), and it is also obvious that such thinking raises difficult questions about internal differentiation and individual unity parallel to those that cropped up in the discussion of the organismic analogy.

CHAPTER 7

1. See, for example, Aquinas's *Summa Theologiae,* gen. ed. Thomas Gilby (Garden City, N.Y.: Doubleday-Image, 1969), 1a, 4, 2 & 3; 1a, 44, 1; 1a, 47, 1 & 2.

2. At different stages of his career, Austin Farrer made imaginative use of each of these two scales of perfection. In *Finite and Infinite,* 2d ed. (London: A. & C. Black, Dacre Press, 1959), he spins out an elaborate and ingenious metaphysic that allows him to express Thomistic-Aristotelian categories in a language drawn from a study of human agency. Farrer understands the indivisible units of existence (i.e., substances) to be units of operation, or activity. He can then translate Thomas's distinction between essence and existence into a distinction between the mode in which activity appears in a particular substance and activity-as-such. Equipped with this distinction, he argues that God can be thought of as perfection in "the character of being an existent" (p. 31). As Farrer develops his metaphysical categories this means that God is absolute activity. "Activity as such has no common distinguishable characteristic; it has, as it were, to realize itself differently in every modification. Where, then, does it realize *itself*? Surely it can somewhere just 'be itself'. This would be its absolute mode" (p. 33).

Farrer later gave up this identification of God with activity-as-such. In *Faith and Speculation* (New York: New York University Press, 1967), he locates God on a scale of agency rather than on a scale of being: God is identified not as absolute activity but as absolute, or sovereign, will. "Such a will can only be defined by its unrestricted freedom" (p. 111). Farrer never systematically explores the nature of this perfect freedom which decisively characterizes the divine agent. Nonetheless, the structure of his argument is clear. Farrer claims that we find both that our own agency is limited in various ways and that these limits are somewhat variable. We can imagine, then, an agent who is free from these limitations, indeed, from every avoidable limitation. "The idea of a will with no given canoe to paddle, so far from being meaningless to us, defines the very goal of our aspiration" (p. 111). Such a will, Farrer suggests, can be said to exemplify agency absolutely.

3. See Nelson Pike's *God and Timelessness*, Studies in Ethics and the Philosophy of Religion (New York: Schocken Books, 1970), chaps. 6-7.

4. It is interesting to note that Austin Farrer retained the notion of divine timelessness when on other issues he turned away from the Neo-Thomist metaphysic of *Finite and Infinite*. In *Faith and Speculation*, Farrer indicates that he intends to "purge out the old Aristotelian leaven" from the theism he developed in his first book; but while he suggests that we conceive of God as Absolute Will, he nonetheless insists upon God's timelessness: "God has neither a past, present, and future, nor will he change" (*Faith and Speculation*, p. 34; see also pp. 95, 139, 164, 169). Farrer links temporality with imperfection in a way that suggests that the purge of Aristotelian (or, more accurately, Neoplatonic) elements from his thinking is not yet complete. He does, however, make some suggestive remarks about the concept of time and the possibility of multiple time orders (*Faith and Speculation*, p. 164).

5. I have not tried to give a full account of the unities that bind together the life of a single agent, though I have pointed to some fundamental structures (see Chap. 5, sec. 4). If that account of agent unity is roughly correct, then clearly the criteria for identity-through-time will not be reducible to criteria for establishing the presence or absence of a self-identical substance; rather, questions about identity-through-time will hinge on judgments about the degrees and kinds of continuity (or discontinuity) that appear within (or break apart) the structure of activity that constitutes an agent's life. We do make such judgments quite effectively in a wide range of cases, but it must be acknowledged that if questions about identity-through-time are inherently complex (i.e., involve balancing a number of considerations that can appear in various combinations), then we may not be able to state precise general criteria that will settle every case in an unproblematic way. Contemporary philosophical literature on identity-through-time has, if nothing else, amply demonstrated this. See, for example: Milton K. Munitz, ed., *Identity and Individuation* (New York: New York University Press, 1971); John Perry, ed., *Personal Identity* (Berkeley and Los Angeles: University of California Press, 1975); Amelie O. Rorty, ed., *The Identities of Persons* (Berkeley and Los Angeles: University of California Press, 1976).

6. In this case, God cannot but be "God." If God were to cease to be perfectly unified, then he would not only cease to be "God" (the perfection of agency) but would also cease to be God (the agent he is); his identity, or continuity, as an enduring individual would be disrupted.

7. See Peter Geach's insistence that promise breaking is not a possible action for God. *Providence and Evil* (Cambridge: Cambridge University Press, 1977), chap. 1, especially p. 19.

8. Richard Swinburne makes an argument of precisely this kind in *The*

Coherence of Theism (Oxford: Oxford University Press, 1977). He argues that if God is omniscient and perfectly free, then it will be incoherent to suggest that he does or could do an action that is on balance more evil than good (see pp. 141-48 and 179ff.). Swinburne's argument hinges on a claim about what it means to say that an agent has a reason for doing an action: "To say that someone judges that he has a reason for doing something is to say that if there are no equally good reasons for not doing that thing and if no factors other than reasons influence him, he will do that thing" (p. 147). Under this definition it is logically inconsistent to say that someone has overriding reasons for performing a particular action, is not influenced by nonrational factors, and yet does not perform that action. As Swinburne makes his case he tends to identify "factors other than reasons" with "causal factors," and he offers "sensual desire and nervous impulses" as examples (p. 148).

This pattern of argument appears to have two odd consequences. First, if evil actions are the result of causal factors that overwhelm rational considerations, then it appears that evil actions are never done freely or responsibly. Second, on this account it appears that actions are either necessary or arbitrary, since good actions are rationally (and therefore logically) necessary, and evil actions are causally necessary. Freedom of choice can appear only as an arbitrary preference between indifferent alternatives. Swinburne comes close to acknowledging this: "His [God's] freedom of choice only operates for choice whether to do an action A when he does not acknowledge overriding reasons for doing A rather than refraining, or for refraining rather than doing A" (p. 148).

9. Perhaps this "circumstantial impossibility" could be reduced to logical impossibility. We might redescribe the action as "bringing about the deposition of the King of France when there is no King of France." This logical inconsistency, however, is generated by joining an internally consistent action description (viz., "bringing about the deposition of the King of France") to an assertion about a state of affairs that is incompatible with it (viz., "there is no King of France"). Hence we can say that this action description is only contingently, or circumstantially, inconsistent.

10. Plantinga, *God and Other Minds* (Ithaca, N.Y.: Cornell University Press, 1967), p. 169.

11. Cf. Aquinas: "Now God considered in himself is altogether one and simple, yet we think of him through a number of different concepts because we cannot see him as he is in himself.

"But although we think of him in these different ways we also know that to each corresponds a single simplicity that is one and the same for all" (*Summa Theologiae,* 1a, 13, 12; see also 1a, 13, 4).

12. See the *Summa Theologiae*, 1a, 12 (especially articles 4 and 11-12) and 1a, 13, 1.

13. See the *Summa Theologiae,* 1a, 4, 2; 1a, 6, 2; 1a, 13, 2. This metaphysical claim lies at the heart of the Thomist account of analogical predication. Given the relation between beings and Being within Aquinas's metaphysical scheme, the positive perfections of creatures can be referred back to God as their source and perfect exemplification. The analogy of proper proportionality, far from fixing exact "values" for the attributes ascribed to God, is simply a formula for expressing the claim that certain creaturely perfections have an unknown analogue within the simple actuality of God's being.

For a fuller presentation of this interpretation of Aquinas and of my own account of God's personal attributes, see my article "The Moral Perfections of God," in *The Thomist,* 47 (1983): 473-500.

14. This theme emerges with great force in *The Divine Relativity: A Social Conception of God* (New Haven: Yale University Press, 1948).

15. Whitehead, *Process and Reality: A Study in Cosmology* (New York: Macmillan, 1929), p. 528.

16. In Whitehead's language, God contributes the initial subjective aim to each actual occasion of experience.

17. Robert Neville, in a detailed and careful study, has pressed this point as a significant objection to process theology. See his *God and Creativity* (New York: The Seabury Press, 1980), especially chaps. 1 and 3.

18. The image of God letting us go out of his hand comes from Kierkegaard's *The Sickness Unto Death*, trans. Walter Lowrie (Princeton: Princeton University Press, 1941), p. 149.

Index